BRAIN GAMES

W9-AXO-452

Sherlock Holmes
Puzzles

Publications International, Ltd.

Let's get social!
@ @Publications_International
@PublicationsInternational
@BrainGames.TM
www.pilbooks.com

Not So Elementary

Do you have what it takes to take on Sherlock Holmes? Be ready to flex every part of your brain as you work through the variety of challenges in this book. Logic puzzles, cryptograms, word searches, memory puzzles, and more will all put your wits, knowledge, and attention to the test.

Whether you're a lifelong admirer of the great detective or a brand-new mystery fiend, an expert puzzler or an absolute newbie, these puzzles offer the challenge for you. If you ever get stuck, take a peek at the answers in the back of the book for a hint.

Now, let's solve a mystery!

Hidden Spot

Below is a quotation from a Sherlock Holmes story. Rearrange each set of scrambled capital letters to reveal the missing word. Bonus: Name the Sherlock Holmes adventure from which this quotation is drawn.

"Now, Watson, now!" cried Holmes with EFRNZDEI _____ eagerness.

All the CNAEMIOALD _____ force of the man EDAMKS _____

behind that SSISETLL _____ manner burst out in a MYPAXSRO

_____ of energy. He tore the drugget from the OFOLR _____, and

in an instant was down on his hands and knees LGCIANW _____

at each of the AQSEUSR _____ of wood beneath it. One turned

DSISWEYA _____ as he dug his nails into the edge of it. It HEDNIG

____ back like the lid of a box. A small black VTIYCA _____ opened

beneath it. Holmes plunged his AEREG _____ hand into it and drew it

out with a bitter NASLR ____ of RNAGE _____ and PTETOMSIANIDPN

_____. It was MYETP _____.

Answers on page 171.

Where the Evidence Leads Us

Cryptograms are messages in substitution code. For example, THE SMART CAT might become FVO QWGDF JGF if F is substituted for **T**, **V** for **H**, **O** for **E**, and so on. Break the code to reveal a quote from a Sherlock Holmes adventure.

TBCTXSVGFMGBFY UIBKUMTU BV F

IUCH GCBTJH GZBMQ. BG SFH VUUS

GW RWBMG IUCH VGCFBQZG GW

WMU GZBMQ, NXG BD HWX VZBDG

HWXC WLM RWBMG WD IBUL F

YBGGYU, HWX SFH DBMK BG

RWBMGBMQ BM FM UPXFYYH

XMTWSRCWSBVBMQ SFMMUC GW

VWSUGZBMQ UMGBCUYH

KBDDUCUMG.

Answers on page 171.

Interception

Sherlock Holmes has intercepted a message that is meant to reveal a location for an upcoming meeting between two criminal masterminds. The only problem is, the message shows many place names. Can you figure out the right location?

ABU DHABI

BARBADOS

ARGENTINA

ICELAND

BEIJING

ALBANIA

SOFIA

ANDORRA

GAMBIA

Answers on page 171.

Say What?

Below is a group of words that, when properly arranged in the blanks, reveal a quote from "A Scandal in Bohemia."

ABHORRENT

BALANCED

COLD

EMOTION

LOVE

It was not that he felt any _____ akin to _____ for Irene Adler. All emotions, and that one particularly, were _____ to his _____, precise, but admirably _____ mind.

Say What?

Below is a group of words that, when properly arranged in the blanks, reveal a quote from the Sherlock Holmes adventure "A Case of Identity."

COMMONPLACES

CONCEIVE

INVENT

MAN

MIND

STRANGER

Life is infinitely _____ than anything which the _____ of _____ could _____. We would not dare to _____ the things which are really mere _____ of existence.

Answers on page 171.

Mysterious Motive

Cryptograms are messages in substitution code. For example, THE SMART CAT might become FVO QWGDF JGF if F is substituted for **T**, V for **H**, O for **E**, and so on. Break the code to reveal a quote from a Sherlock Holmes adventure.

"FOZN VJ NOB UBZTVTP SG VN, FZNJST?" JZVW

OSRUBJ JSRBUTRC ZJ OB RZVW WSFT NOB

MZMBH. "FOZN SYEBXN VJ JBHKBW YC NOVJ

XVHXRB SG UVJBHC ZTW KVSRBTXB ZTW GBZH?

VN ULJN NBTW NS JSUB BTW, SH BRJB SLH LTVK-

BHJB VJ HLRBW YC XOZTXB, FOVXO VJ LTNOVTI-

ZYRB. YLN FOZN BTW? NOBHB VJ NOB PHBZN

JNZTWVTP MBHBTTVZR MHSYRBU NS FOVXO

OLUZT HBZJST VJ ZJ GZH GHSU ZT ZTJFBH ZJ

BKBH."

– NOB ZWKBTNLHB SG NOB XZHWYSZHW YSD

Read the story below, then turn the page and answer the questions.

The detective overheard the jewelry thief tell his accomplice about the different places where he stashed the loot. He said, "The diamond is in the canister full of loose tea. The emerald is in the refill bottle of liquid soap in the half bathroom. The ruby is inside the winter boot in the hall closet. The garnet ring is taped to the back of the spice rack."

Overheard Information (Part II)

(Do not read this until you have read the previous page!)

The detective overheard the information about where the stolen loot was stored, but didn't have anywhere to write it down! Answer the questions below to help him remember.

1. The diamond is found in a canister containing this.

   A. Tea

   B. Coffee beans

   C. Spices

   D. Soap

2. What is found taped to the spice rack?

   A. Diamond

   B. Emerald

   C. Ruby

   D. Garnet

3. The ruby is found here.

   A. A shoe in the bedroom closet.

   B. A winter boot in the bedroom closet.

   C. A winter boot in the hall closet.

   D. A sneaker in the hall closet.

4. The emerald is found here.

   A. A bottle of liquid soap.

   B. A bottle of liquid shampoo.

   C. A bottle of laundry detergent.

   D. In the bathroom, but we don't know a more specific location.

Answers on page 172.

The Murderous Gem Thief

5 types of gems were stolen from the murder scene. There was 1 gem of the first type, 2 of the second type, 3 of the third type, 4 of the fourth type, and 5 of the fifth type. From the information given below, can you tell how many gemstones of each kind were taken?

1. There is one more garnet than amethyst.

2. There are at least two more peridots than diamonds.

3. Rubies are neither the most rare nor most plentiful gem.

4. There are more amethysts than diamonds.

5. There are two more garnets than rubies.

Answers on page 172.

Dramatic Entrance

Every word or phrase in all capital letters is contained within the group of letters. Words can be found in a straight line horizontally, vertically, or diagonally. They may be read either forward or backward.

We have had some DRAMATIC entrances and EXITS upon our small STAGE at BAKER STREET, but I cannot RECOLLECT anything more SUDDEN and STARTLING than the first APPEARANCE of THORNEYCROFT Huxtable, M.A., Ph.D., etc. His card, which SEEMED too small to carry the WEIGHT of his academic DISTINCTIONS, preceded him by a few SECONDS, and then he entered himself—so large, so POMPOUS, and so DIGNIFIED that he was the very EMBODIMENT of self-possession and SOLIDITY. And yet his first ACTION, when the DOOR had closed behind him, was to STAGGER against the table, whence he SLIPPED down upon the floor, and there was that MAJESTIC figure PROSTRATE and INSENSIBLE upon our BEARSKIN hearthrug.

– The Adventure of the Priory School

```
Y D Q P A N Q D D I G N I F I E D I E E
N E F W O T E I F L C H L R Q L A N M L
Y J T I S M H G Y I Y T X S N U K R B B
J P T A E O L O T P E D E D Q F W B O I
W C O E R E L S R E H C H E X B N E D S
A V S M O T E I R N O Q Y X H B N A I N
S U W K P J S T D N E I O I Z Z N R M E
U T T G A O S O D I Z Y T T Y G E S E S
T F A M P R U S R N T U C S C U R K N N
C U U G E L P S O P F Y Q R L V O I T I
E W F K E F D R A M A T I C O K O N U O
L X A A T H S L I P P E D A I F D X C W
L B P A P P E A R A N C E U F D T K O P
O T S E T N P R S N O I T C N I T S I D
C O Q X O H N K E N T Q M G P S G Q H L
E I Y L R W G S Y G E D S Z O K B R I C
R H P W U L J I N S G D R A X J D X Y E
T R U J F N C C E O Z A D E S T G J L D
I Y C E V A A E Z W J A T U E Y N M P J
K C G N I L T R A T S W H S S U Q M W Q
```

13

Answers on page 172.

Baker Street Revisited

ACROSS

1. Chunk, as of concrete
5. Melodic motif
10. Word before Kitchen or Angels
12. Faced courageously
13. Of feathered friends
14. Not at all well
15. 1988 British comedy with Michael Caine as Sherlock
17. One way to be missed
18. At the stern
21. Brit's 26th letter
22. Done with
26. "The Woman," to Holmes
28. "West Side Story" girlfriend
29. Talkative bird
30. "Life of Pi" director Lee
32. Superb serve
33. Fable messages
36. 1979 "memoir" about adventures of Sherlock's brother, Mycroft Holmes
42. Major arteries
43. Airline seat choice
44. Agreement between nations
45. Blends or combines
46. Drawn-out battle
47. Place for a chin on a violin

DOWN

1. "Pygmalion" author
2. Big name in jeans
3. Got down from a horse
4. Down feeling, with "the"
5. Courtroom drama, e.g.
6. ___ days (happy time in the past)
7. Devil's specialty
8. Bill of fare
9. Jigsaw puzzle solver's starting point, often
11. Clock-radio button
12. With ___ breath (expectantly)
16. "If I Was" singer Midge
18. Align the crosshairs
19. Fish banquet
20. Gymnast's perfect score
23. By way of
24. List-ending abbr.
25. "Boy Problems" singer Carly ___ Jepsen
27. It may say "Hello"
28. Lustrous, poetically
30. Pretentious, as a film
31. "I'll have to pass"
34. Deliver a speech
35. More crafty
36. Diner sign
37. Edible seaweed used for sushi
38. Ancestry diagram
39. Getaway spot in the sea
40. Cutlass or 88, in the auto world
41. Chicks' hangout?

1	2	3	4				5	6	7	8	9
10				11		12					
13						14					
15					16						
			17								
18	19	20		21				22	23	24	25
26			27				28				
29					30	31			32		
			33	34				35			
36	37	38							39	40	41
42						43					
44						45					
46							47				

15

Answers on page 172.

Interception

Sherlock Holmes has intercepted a message that is meant to reveal a location for an upcoming meeting between two criminal masterminds. The only problem is, the message shows many place names. Can you figure out the right location?

RABAT

GHENT

YAREN

MALTA

QUITO

TUNIS

Answers on page 172.

Study this picture for one minute, then turn the page.

What Changed? (Part II)

(Do not read this until you have read the previous page!)

Murder by stabbing! From memory, can you tell what changed between this and the previous page to pinpoint what was used as a weapon?

Answers on page 172.

The Adventure of the Blue Carbuncle (Part I)

Sherlock Holmes learned the information below while trying to solve a mystery. Read the text, then turn the page for a quiz on what you've read.

John Horner, 26, plumber, was brought up upon the charge of having upon the 22nd inst., abstracted from the jewel-case of the Countess of Morcar the valuable gem known as the blue carbuncle. James Ryder, upper-attendant at the hotel, gave his evidence to the effect that he had shown Horner up to the dressing room of the Countess of Morcar upon the day of the robbery in order that he might solder the second bar of the grate, which was loose. He had remained with Horner some little time, but had finally been called away. On returning, he found that Horner had disappeared, that the bureau had been forced open, and that the small morocco casket in which, as it afterwards transpired, the Countess was accustomed to keep her jewel, was lying empty upon the dressing table.

The Adventure of the Blue Carbuncle (Part II)

(Do not read this until you have read the previous page!)

1. What was John Horner's occupation?

   A. Plumber

   B. Upper-attendant

   C. Valet

   D. Butler

2. Why was a plumber brought to the burgled hotel room?

   A. To fix the water pipes

   B. To fix a leaky faucet

   C. To solder the bar of a grate

   D. To interview for a new job

3. What did Ryder find forced open?

   A. A small morocco casket

   B. The bureau

   C. The dressing room door

   D. The dressing table

4. What is the title of the woman who owned the blue carbuncle?

   A. Lady

   B. Honorable

   C. Countess

   D. Duchess

Answers on page 173.

Domestic Logic

On Box Street, there are 5 adjacent houses that are identical to each other. You've been asked to visit Mr. Linus, but without any addresses on the doors you are not sure which house to approach. At the local coffee shop, you ask the waitress for help. She is able to provide the following information:

A. Mr. Linus does not like dogs.

B. The dog living next door to Mr. Linus often tunnels under his other neighbor's fence to chase their cat.

C. There are no animals at House B.

D. House A owns a cat.

E. House C owns a cat.

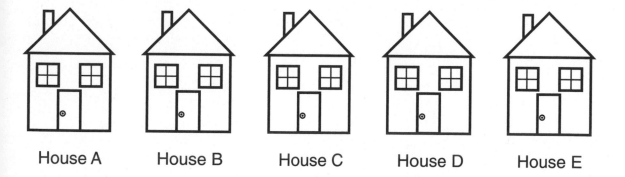

House A   House B   House C   House D   House E

Answers on page 173.

Mycroft Holmes

1. In what story do we first meet Mycroft?

    A. The Final Problem

    B. The Greek Interpreter

    C. The Adventure of the Empty House

    D. A Study in Scarlet

2. Mycroft is ___ years ___ than Sherlock

    A. 7 years younger

    B. 3 years older

    C. 7 years older

    D. 3 years younger

3. Mycroft founded which London gentleman's club?

    A. Alpine

    B. Diogenes

    C. Athenaeum

    D. Caledonian

4. Which of these actors has NOT portrayed Mycroft on screen?

    A. Laurence Olivier

    B. Mark Gatiss

    C. Rhys Ifans

    D. Stephen Fry

Answers on page 173.

Shades of Red

Below is a quotation from a Sherlock Holmes story. Rearrange each set of scrambled capital letters to reveal the missing word. Bonus: Name the Sherlock Holmes adventure from which this quotation is drawn.

From north, south, east, and west every man who had a DSEHA _____ of red in his hair had PARTMED _____ into the city to WSAENR _____ the IAEDENTMRTVSE _____. Fleet Street was HEDCOK _____ with red-headed folk, and Pope's ORUCT _____ looked like a coster's orange ORBAWR _____. I should not have thought there were so many in the whole OUTNYCR _____ as were brought EROTGETH _____ by that single ENEMRAVSTDTIE _____. Every shade of color they were—straw, OMLNE _____, orange, BKIRC _____, Irish-setter, VIELR _____, clay.

Answers on page 173.

Pick Your Poison

There are five bottles before you, but they've gotten jumbled up. Poison is found in one of them. If you arrange them from left to right, following the instructions given below, you will be able to know where the poison is found.

1. The poison is found in either the far left, middle, or far right positions.

2. The poison is found in neither the largest nor the smallest bottle.

3. The three medium-size sized bottles are found in a row.

4. At least one bottle separates the largest and smallest bottles.

Answers on page 173.

Cryptograms are messages in substitution code. For example, THE SMART CAT might become FVO QWGDF JGF if **F** is substituted for **T**, **V** for **H**, **O** for **E**, and so on. Break the code to reveal a quote from a Sherlock Holmes adventure.

"AG VCPU JPZQIR," QPSV EC, "S NPRRIZ

POUCC JSZE ZEIQC JEI UPRT AIVCQZG

PAIRO ZEC KSUZLCQ. ZI ZEC BIOSNSPR

PBB ZESROQ QEILBV DC QCCR CHPNZBG

PQ ZECG PUC, PRV ZI LRVCUCQZSAPZC

IRC'Q QCBX SQ PQ ALNE P VCMPUZLUC

XUIA ZULZE PQ ZI CHPOOCUPZC IRC'Q

IJR MIJCUQ. JECR S QPG, ZECUCXIUC,

ZEPZ AGNUIXZ EPQ DCZZCU MIJCUQ IX

IDQCUKPZSIR ZEPR S, GIL APG ZPTC SZ

ZEPZ S PA QMCPTSRO ZEC CHPNZ PRV

BSZCUPB ZULZE."

– ZEC OUCCT SRZCUMUCZCU

25

Answers on page 173.

Criminals

How many kinds of criminals can you find here? We count 8. To spell out a criminal, keep moving from one letter to the next in any direction—up, down, across, or diagonally. You may move in several different directions for each word. You can also use letters more than once—but not in the same word.

```
M   O   B   B   O   O

T   U   R   E   R   K

B   L   G   G   T   C

R   A   G   S   I   H

W   I   N   D   E   F
```

Find the matching fingerprint(s). There may be more than one.

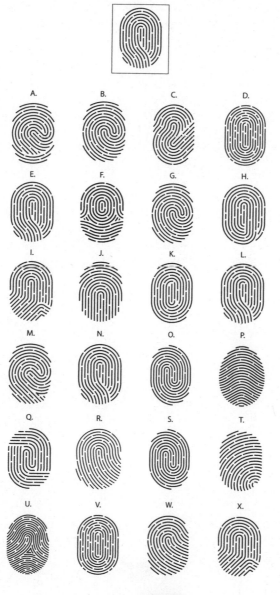

Answers on page 174.

Collection of Cases

Every word or phrase in all capital letters is contained within the group of letters. Words can be found in a straight line horizontally, vertically, or diagonally. They may be read either forward or backward.

The year '87 FURNISHED us with a long series of CASES of greater or less INTEREST, of which I retain the RECORDS. Among my HEADINGS under this one twelve months I find an ACCOUNT of the adventure of the PARADOL Chamber, of the Amateur MENDICANT Society, who held a LUXURIOUS club in the lower VAULT of a furniture WAREHOUSE, of the facts CONNECTED with the loss of the British BAROQUE Sophy Anderson, of the SINGULAR adventures of the Grice PATERSONS in the island of UFFA, and finally of the Camberwell POISONING case. In the latter, as may be REMEMBERED, Sherlock Holmes was able, by WINDING up the dead man's WATCH, to prove that it had been wound up two HOURS before, and that therefore the DECEASED had gone to bed within that time—a DEDUCTION which was of the GREATEST importance in CLEARING up the case.

– The Five Orange Pips

```
O J Y D O I A X T R P P U D F Y V N
C E Z E S U Y V E H B A R O Q U E S
T K X C L R D M O R H R V J Q P H E
N Z Q E B Q E U A U Z A F T U O D S
U I B A T M R L D B I D M D W I E A
O D Y S B S U E N B U O J J B S T C
C W E E R G H U E U N L B J T O C Y
C Q R D N S M E N D I C A N T N E B
A E J I I D E D U C T I O N B I N C
D C S N W G N I D N I W S X G N N S
F Y R B C I K S L I W P Q R J G O U
L U N N O O D Y N S B H T V C O C O
F S N O S R E T R A P X U F F A Q I
S D X M O T E J W G R E A T E S T R
M Q K C L R E G N I R A E L C N Q U
K C E U E Y S M D H E A D I N G S X
X R A S D L E S U O H E R A W Z E U
C V T J F Z W Z E W A T C H D V T L
```

29

Answers on page 174.

Moriarty Appears

Below is a quotation from a Sherlock Holmes story. Rearrange each set of scrambled capital letters to reveal the missing word. Bonus: Name the Sherlock Holmes adventure from which this quotation is drawn.

"He is MLXREYEET _____ tall and thin, his REDAHFOE _____ domes out in a white VERCU _____, and his two eyes are deeply sunken in his head. He is clean-shaven, pale, and CCEIAST ____-looking, retaining EONITMHSG _____ of the RSPFSREOO _____ in his features. His DHROSESUL _____ are UDRNOED _____ from much study, and his face DUEOTRRSP _____ forward, and is forever slowly AINCTLIGLOS _____ from side to side in a curiously LETRNPIIA _____ fashion. He peered at me with great TYORICUIS _____ in his DECUPEKR _____ eyes."

Answers on page 174.

Read the story below, then turn the page and answer the questions.

While on a train, a bystander overheard a criminal tell an accomplice about an upcoming set of crimes. The criminal said, "We don't need you for the hit on the grocery store on the 20th, but we need a getaway driver for the next day. We're going back to that music store on Pearson Street, you know the one. And then we're going to that little diner on Fourth Street next weekend while our mutual friend is bussing tables so he can help us out."

Overheard Information (Part II)

(Do not read this until you have read the previous page!)

The bystander overheard the information about the crimes that were planned, but didn't have anywhere to write it down! Answer the questions below to help the bystander remember what to tell the police.

1. The hit on the music store will take place on this day.

   A. The 20th

   B. The 21st

   C. Next weekend

   D. A day is not specified.

2. The grocery store is found on this street.

   A. Pearson Street

   B. Fourth Street

   C. Main Street

   D. A location is not given.

3. The thief asks his accomplice to be a getaway driver for the hit on the grocery store.

   A. True

   B. False

4. The thieves will have a man on the inside at this location.

   A. Grocery store

   B. Music store

   C. Diner

   D. None of the above

Answers on page 174.

Sherlock Holmes learned the information below while trying to solve a mystery. Read the text, then turn the page for a quiz on what you've read.

The ceremony, which was performed at St. George's, Hanover Square, was a very quiet one, no one being present save the father of the bride, Mr. Aloysius Doran, the Duchess of Balmoral, Lord Backwater, Lord Eustace and Lady Clara St. Simon (the younger brother and sister of the bridegroom), and Lady Alicia Whittington. The whole party proceeded afterwards to the house of Mr. Aloysius Doran, at Lancaster Gate, where breakfast had been prepared. It appears that some little trouble was caused by a woman, whose name has not been ascertained, who endeavored to force her way into the house after the bridal party, alleging that she had some claim upon Lord St. Simon.

The Adventure of the Noble Bachelor (Part II)

(Do not read this until you have read the previous page!)

1. Where was the ceremony performed?

    A. Lancaster Gate

    B. Balmoral

    C. Hanover Square

    D. Whittington

2. How many people attended the wedding?

    A. Five

    B. Six

    C. Seven

    D. Ten

3. Who was the younger brother of the bridegroom?

    A. Lord Eustace

    B. Mr. Aloysius Doran

    C. Mr. St. George

    D. Lord St. Simon

4. What meal had been prepared for the bridal party after the wedding?

    A. Breakfast

    B. Lunch

    C. Tea

    D. Dinner

Answers on page 174.

The Murderous Gem Thief

5 types of gems were stolen from the murder scene. There was 1 gem of the first type, 2 of the second type, 3 of the third type, 4 of the fourth type, and 5 of the fifth type. From the information given below, can you tell how many gemstones of each kind were taken?

1. There are an even number of diamonds.

2. There are at least two pieces of topaz.

3. There are more rubies than sapphires.

4. There are three more rubies than there are pieces of turquoise.

5. There are more pieces of topaz than rubies.

Answers on page 175.

The Cost of Secrets

Below is a quotation from a Sherlock Holmes story. Rearrange each set of scrambled capital letters to reveal the missing word.

"Well, my dear sir, INNGKWO _____ the ECIDITVNVI _____ character of his old SASISEACTO _____, he was trying to hide his own YENTIIDT _____ from YYEBROEDV _____ as long as he could. His secret was a SELAMFUH ____ one, and he could not bring himself to UELDGVI _____ it. However, HECWRT _____ as he was, he was still living under the shield of TRHBISI _____ law, and I have no doubt, ORITPSENC _____, that you will see that, though that LHDIES _____ may fail to guard, the ROSWD _____ of UEJITSC _____ is still there to avenge."

— The SNERDIET _____ Patient

Cryptograms are messages in substitution code. For example, THE SMART CAT might become FVO QWGDF JGF if **F** is substituted for **T**, **V** for **H**, **O** for **E**, and so on. Break the code to reveal a quote from a Sherlock Holmes adventure.

VI KWTUIG BWAH HVI ZNFZV HN HVI

NBIQ KYQGNK, WQG VITG FB HVI

GMNNBYQR AHWTU NE W SNAA-

MNAI, TNNUYQR GNKQ WH HVI GWY-

QHD PTIQG NE ZMYSANQ WQG

RMIIQ. YH KWA W QIK BVWAI NE VYA

ZVWMWZHIM HN SI, ENM Y VWG

QILIM PIENMI AIIQ VYS AVNK WQD

UIIQ YQHIMIAH YQ QWHFMWT

NPXIZHA.

– HVI QWLWT HMIWHD

Answers on page 175.

The detective found a list that the burglar left behind. She knows that the burglar likes to scramble words, then remove one letter. To help the detective, discover the missing letter, then unscramble the words. When you do, you'll reveal the burglar's plans on a specific city and day, as well as his method of transport.

ERRED PUT

RIPS

DYED NEWS

PRALINE

Dr. Watson made the observations below while he and Sherlock Holmes were trying to solve a mystery. Read the text, then turn the page for a quiz on what you've read.

The study proved to be a small chamber, lined on three sides with books, and with a writing table facing an ordinary window, which looked out upon the garden. Our first attention was given to the body of the unfortunate squire, whose huge frame lay stretched across the room. His disordered dress showed that he had been hastily aroused from sleep. The bullet had been fired at him from the front, and had remained in his body, after penetrating the heart. His death had certainly been instantaneous and painless. There was no powder-marking either upon his dressing-gown or on his hands. According to the country surgeon, the lady had stains upon her face, but none upon her hand.

The Adventure of the Dancing Men (Part II)

(Do not read this until you have read the previous page!)

1. In which room of the house was the body found?

    A. Dining room

    B. Entryway

    C. Bedroom

    D. Study

2. The victim's disordered state of dress indicated what fact?

    A. He had been in a fight

    B. He did not care about his appearance

    C. He had been hastily woken from sleep

    D. He had just arrived at the house

3. From which direction had the squire been shot?

    A. Front

    B. Back

    C. Left

    D. Right

4. The bullet had hit which part of the victim's body?

    A. Arm

    B. Head

    C. Stomach

    D. Heart

Answers on page 175.

Train Station Terrors

The Trixster has hidden a stolen briefcase full of diamonds in one of forty-five different lockers at the train station. Each locker has a different number, and the miscreant has given the police a series of clues that will point to its hidden location. Can you find the diamonds?

1. It is odd.

2. It is divisible by 3.

3. The second digit is greater than 6.

4. The sum of the digits is less than 10.

11	12	13	14	15	16	17	18	19
21	22	23	24	25	26	27	28	29
31	32	33	34	35	36	37	38	39
41	42	43	44	45	46	47	48	49
51	52	53	54	55	56	57	58	59

41

Answers on page 175.

On the Scent

Every word or phrase in all capital letters is contained within the group of letters. Words can be found in a straight line horizontally, vertically, or diagonally. They may be read either forward or backward.

I could tell by numerous SUBTLE signs, which might have been LOST upon anyone but MYSELF, that HOLMES was on a HOT SCENT. As IMPASSIVE as ever to the CASUAL observer, there were none the less a subdued EAGERNESS and suggestion of TENSION in his BRIGHTENED eyes and BRISKER manner which ASSURED me that the GAME was AFOOT. After his HABIT he said nothing, and after mine I asked no QUESTIONS. Sufficient for me to share the SPORT and lend my HUMBLE help to the CAPTURE without distracting that INTENT brain with needless INTERRUPTION. All would come round to me in DUE TIME.

– The Adventure of Wisteria Lodge

```
B P T O L U D E R U S S A Q M S V B
U X A Y C P E T D T T J R W Y E F F
Q K Y Y Z U P L E Q C E I O S M N B
U E J A K E E N T H G N A K E L R I
E E K M M B S M B B T Y F X L O K U
S A R A X I G B I E U Z O T F H D B
T Q G M O R I L R T K S O N H S J L
I S J N W N I R S L E Z T E K X B H
O P G M T C U F W U R U W C M U R J
N B L E V P A D E E Y H D S U I I I
S T N O T B X S V A J K K T L Z S A
M T C I S I Y I U E G U W O T T K V
Y H O T X T S L L A Q E D H B E E M
T N A M R S U B N L L W R T A B R H
S Y N B A O M E X U O E E N E V J Q
J B J P I U P Q B R I G H T E N E D
Z E M J H T P S I D H Y R D E S Y S
D I C A P T U R E T B D B J O D S T
```

43

Answers on page 176.

Say What?

Below is a group of words that, when properly arranged in the blanks, reveal a quote from the Sherlock Holmes adventure "A Case of Identity."

COINCIDENCES

FICTION

FLY

FORESEEN

GENERATIONS

GREAT

HOVER

PEEP

WONDERFUL

If we could _____ out of that window hand in hand, _____ over this _____ city, gently remove the roofs, and _____ in at the queer things which are going on, the strange _____, the plannings, the cross-purposes, the _____ chains of events, working through _____, and leading to the most outré results, it would make all _____ with its conventionalities and _____ conclusions most stale and unprofitable.

Answers on page 176.

Fingerprint Match

Find one or more fingerprints that match the one in the box.

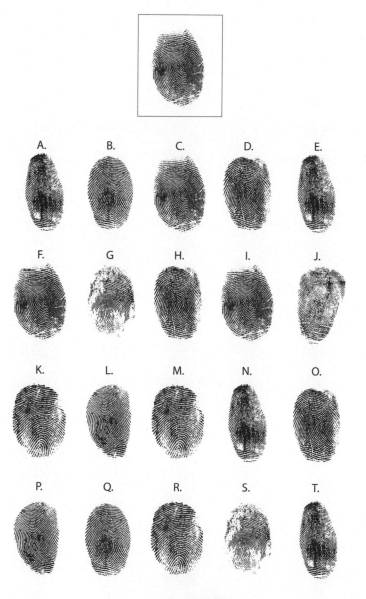

Answers on page 176.

Holmes on His Own

Below is a quotation from a Sherlock Holmes story. Rearrange each set of scrambled capital letters to reveal the missing word. Bonus: Name the Sherlock Holmes adventure from which this quotation is drawn.

I had seen little of Holmes lately. My RAIAGRME _____ had drifted us away from each other. My own complete NISPHESPA ____, and the home-centered ERTSTIENS _____ which rise up around the man who first finds himself master of his own TTEIALHSENBMS _____, were sufficient to absorb all my attention, while Holmes, who HTLDEOA _____ every form of society with his whole ENBAMOIH _____ soul, remained in our lodgings in Baker Street, buried among his old books, and alternating from week to week between cocaine and ANMBITOI _____, the RSWSDOINSE _____ of the drug, and the fierce energy of his own keen nature. He was still, as ever, deeply RDTTATACE _____ by the study of crime, and occupied his immense CELITFUSA _____ and RAODYTARIREXN _____ powers of observation in following out those clues, and clearing up those SMSIEREYT _____ which had been DANONABED _____ as ESHPSELO _____ by the official police.

46

Sherlock's Retirement

1. To what location does Sherlock Holmes retire?

   A. Sussex Downs

   B. Pall Mall

   C. Cambridge

   D. East Norfolk

2. What is Holmes' retirement hobby?

   A. Gardening

   B. Beekeeping

   C. Fossil hunting

   D. Birdwatching

3. In what book to we learn about Holmes' retirement?

   A. The Memoirs of Sherlock Holmes

   B. The Valley of Fear

   C. The Case-Book of Sherlock Holmes

   D. His Last Bow

4. Of what nature are the "occasional attacks" Holmes suffers in retirement?

   A. Nostalgia

   B. Boredom

   C. Rheumatism

   D. Former enemies

Coded Letter

This message came for Sherlock Holmes, but the writer used a substitution code. For example, THE SMART CAT might become FVO QWGDF JGF if **F** is substituted for **T**, **V** for **H**, **O** for **E**, and so on. Break the code to reveal the message. Bonus question: What Sherlock Holmes story includes this letter?

GZ DYN JGAA YBAD MYSP XYNBV KL

RNKXLPX LY LJPAFP

LY LTP PKQL EKLP DYN JGAA APKXB

JTKL

JGAA FPXD SNMT QNXUXGQP DYN

KBV SKDWP

WP YZ LTP EXPKLPQL QPXFGMP LY

DYN KBV KAQY

LY KBBGP SYXXGQYB. WNL QKD

BYLTGBE LY KBDYBP/ NUYB LTP

SKLLPX

48

Treasure Hunt

Sherlock Holmes is tracking a jewelry thief's past trips in order to find and recover jewelry that was left behind in six cities. Each city was visited only once. Can you put together the travel timeline, using the information below?

1. The trip began and ended in the two cities closest to the equator.

2. The two cities in Europe were not visited back to back.

3. The thief visited New York City sometime before Bogata.

4. After visiting London, the thief visited one other city before visiting Nairobi.

5. Singapore was visited sometime before Paris.

Answers on page 177.

Which Adventure?

Match each event with the Sherlock Holmes adventure in which it occurs.

1. Moriarty's introduction

2. Holmes returns after being thought dead

3. Holmes and Watson meet

4. Irene Adler's introduction

A. A Scandal in Bohemia

B. The Adventure of the Empty House

C. A Study in Scarlet

D. The Final Solution

Answers on page 177.

Dr. Watson made the observations below while he and Sherlock Holmes were trying to solve a mystery. Read the text, then turn the page for a quiz on what you've read.

I was, of course, familiar with the pictures of the famous Duke, but the man himself was very different from his representation. He was a tall and stately person, scrupulously dressed, with a drawn, thin face, and a nose which was grotesquely curved and long. His complexion was of a dead pallor, which was more startling by contrast with a long, dwindling beard of vivid red, which flowed down over his white waistcoat with his watch-chain gleaming through its fringe. Such was the stately presence who looked stonily at us from the center of Dr. Huxtable's hearthrug. Beside him stood a very young man, whom I understood to be Wilder, the private secretary. He was small, nervous, alert with intelligent light-blue eyes and mobile features.

The Adventure of the Priory School (Part II)

(Do not read this until you have read the previous page!)

1. What color was the Duke's beard?

    A. Black

    B. Gray

    C. Red

    D. Blond

2. What color was the Duke's waist-coat?

    A. White

    B. Black

    C. Checkered

    D. Red

3. What was Wilder's assumed occupation?

    A. Valet

    B. Business owner

    C. Assistant manager

    D. Secretary

4. What shape was the Duke's nose?

    A. Thin

    B. Curved

    C. Bulbous

    D. Straight

Answers on page 177.

The Reigate Squires

Choose the correct word or phrase to complete each quote from a Sherlock Holmes adventure.

1. A stone-flagged passage, with the _____ branching away from it, led by a wooden staircase directly to the first floor of the house.

   A. Servant's quarters

   B. Kitchens

   C. Cellars

   D. Bedrooms

2. It came out upon the landing opposite to a second more _____ stair which came up from the front hall.

   A. Ornamental

   B. Sturdy

   C. Curved

   D. Interesting

3. Holmes walked slowly, taking keen note of the _____ of the house.

   A. Intricacies

   B. Decorations

   C. Damages

   D. Architecture

4. I could tell from his expression that he was on a _____, and yet I could not in the least imagine in what direction his inferences were leading him.

   A. Trail

   B. Mission

   C. Hot scent

   D. Distraction

Answers on page 177.

This puzzle functions exactly like an anagram with an added step: In addition to being scrambled, each word below is missing the same letter. Discover the missing letter, then unscramble the words to reveal five terms related to crime scene investigation.

LOSE

NEED ICE

EAT SING TIE

TEE EDICT

HE TIES

Crime Cryptogram

Cryptograms are messages in substitution code. Break the code to read the message. For example, THE SMART CAT might become FVO QWGDF JGF if **F** is substituted for **T**, **V** for **H**, **O** for **E**, and so on.

ZNK GIZUX'Y IUYZGX GIIAYKJ NOS UL G

JGYZGXJRE IXOSK, HAZ ZNK VUROIK XKLAYKJ ZU

OTBKYZOMGZK. CNGZ JOJ NK JU?

NK YZURK ZNK YIKTK!

Answers on page 177.

Mysterious Force

Below is a quotation from a Sherlock Holmes story. Rearrange each set of scrambled capital letters to reveal the missing word. Bonus: Name the Sherlock Holmes adventure from which this quotation is drawn.

"As you are aware, Watson, there is no one who knows the RIHGEH

_____ criminal world of ONONDL _____ so well as I do. For years past I

have UTLLANYCNIO _____ been CISSNUCOO _____ of some power

behind the MREFLTACAO _____, some deep NNORIGZGIA _____ pow-

er which RREVOFE _____ stands in the way of the law and throws its

LEDHIS _____ over the wrong doer. Again and again in cases of the most

varying sorts—OYRRGEF _____ cases, BREIOEBRS _____, MUDSRRE

_____ – I have felt the presence of this force, and I have deduced its ac-

tion in many of those UEDEOCVDRINS _____ crimes in which I have not

been personally SCUTDLOEN _____. For years I have VDAEENEDOR

_____ to break through the veil which shrouded it, and at last the time

came when I seized my DAEHTR _____ and followed it, until it led me,

after a thousand cunning NIISWDGN _____, to ex-Professor Moriarty of

HMTAITLEAMCA _____ celebrity.

Answers on page 178.

Below is a group of words that, when properly arranged in the blanks, reveal a quote from the Sherlock Holmes story "The Adventure of the Speckled Band."

ADMIRING

DEDUCTIONS

FOUNDED

INTUITIONS

KEENER

LOGICAL

PROFESSIONAL

SUBMITTED

UNRAVELED

I had no _____ pleasure than in following Holmes in his _____ investigations, and in _____ the rapid _____, as swift as _____, and yet always founded on a _____ basis, with which he _____ the problems which were _____ to him.

Answers on page 178.

Pick Your Poison

There are five bottles before you, but they've gotten jumbled up. Poison is found in one of them. If you arrange them from left to right, following the instructions given below, you will be able to know where the poison is found.

1. The bottles are red, orange, yellow, green, and blue, but not necessarily in that order.

2. The poison is in a bottle with a primary color.

3. The yellow bottle is either in the middle or on the far right.

4. The blue bottle is either the far left bottle or the one next to it.

5. The orange bottle is to the immediate left of the bottle with the poison.

6. The red bottle is the furthest to the right.

7. The green bottle and the blue bottle are separated by one other bottle.

57

Answers on page 178.

Motel Hideout

A thief hides out in one of the 45 motel rooms listed in the chart below. Sherlock Holmes received a sheet of four clues, signed "The Logical Thief." Using these clues, the detective found the room number within 15 minutes—but by that time, the thief had fled. Can you find the thief's motel room quicker?

1. It is a prime number larger than 20.

2. The second digit is larger than the first.

3. The second digit is divisible by 3.

4. The first digit is not divisible by 2.

51	52	53	54	55	56	57	58	59
41	42	43	44	45	46	47	48	49
31	32	33	34	35	36	37	38	39
21	22	23	24	25	26	27	28	29
11	12	13	14	15	16	17	18	19

Answers on page 178.

Sherlock Holmes intercepted a message. He thinks it might be the location of a meeting between two criminals, but it doesn't seem to make sense. Can you decipher the true message?

CELERY TOO TWO OAT AGAIN GAZING EARTHWARDS

FIXING RIVER ZOO VEER VANE

IS SOON NEW

NEAR OVAL BOO MOVE

WANE ILL RIG HAT PAT

Answers on page 178.

When Holmes Is Bored

Below is a quotation from a Sherlock Holmes adventure. Every word or phrase in all capital letters is contained within the group of letters. Words can be found in a straight line horizontally, vertically, or diagonally. They may be read either forward or backward.

In the third week of NOVEMBER, in the year 1895, a DENSE yellow fog SETTLED down upon LONDON. From the Monday to the Thursday, I DOUBT whether it was ever possible from our windows in BAKER STREET to see the LOOM of the opposite houses. The first day Holmes had spent in CROSS-INDEXING his huge book of REFERENCES. The second and third had been PATIENTLY occupied upon a SUBJECT which he had recently made his HOBBY—the music of the MIDDLE AGES. But when, for the fourth time, after PUSHING back our chairs from BREAKFAST we saw the GREASY, heavy brown SWIRL still DRIFTING past us and CONDENSING in oily drops upon the WINDOWPANES, my comrade's IMPATIENT and ACTIVE nature could ENDURE this drab EXISTENCE no longer.

– The Adventure of the Bruce-Partington Plans

60

```
H G M D G C D N O V E M B E R I R E
T O P E K R W Q D E N S E H Z E B T
B C B I F O E P I H T I M F F B M U
U M L B F S Z A P V G K S E W B T Q
O U S W Y S B T S Q A H R X T V T U
D V W E I I S G N Y I E Z P Q C B B
T Q I X H N L E D E N M A P E U T P
S T R I R D D S G C I T N J O R E L
A L L S D E I O E A I T B W F F E G
F E S T R X H S W E E U A G L A R N
K F N E I I A C N P S L M P C X T I
A J O N F N O T M N A J D T M X S H
E A D C T G L E Z O T N I D U I R S
R X N E I Y S F Y U O V E W I V E U
B J O K N F V A W N E L H S I M K P
K J L V G N E R U D N E Y G S X A O
O Q E E G N I S N E D N O C R Q B V
F E D Y Y F S E T T L E D W M K C P
```

61

Answers on page 178.

Most Unusual

Below is a group of words that, when properly arranged in the blanks, reveal a quote from a Sherlock Holmes story.

FEATURELESS

IDENTIFY

BIZARRE

COMMONPLACE

COMMONPLACE

MYSTERIOUS

"As a rule," said Holmes, "the more ___ a thing is, the less ____ it proves to be. It is your ___, ___ crimes which are really puzzling, just as a ___ face is the most difficult to ____."

– The Red-Headed League

Answers on page 179.

Treasure Hunt

The treasure hunter found six treasures in a row. At each find, she found a clue for the next treasure. Can you put the list of the six treasures she found in order, using the information below?

1. The amethysts were one of the first two finds, and were found earlier than the diamonds, the rubies, or the sapphires.

2. The diamonds were not the final find.

3. The silver coins were found immediately after the gold bars, and sometime before the diamonds, but not immediately before.

4. Exactly two other finds separated the amethysts and the rubies.

Answers on page 179.

Holmes Books

Match each Sherlock Holmes book with its year of publication.

1. A Study in Scarlet

2. The Adventures of Sherlock Holmes

3. The Sign of Four

4. The Return of Sherlock Holmes

A. 1905

B. 1887

C. 1892

D. 1890

Answers on page 179.

Study this picture for one minute, then turn the page.

(Do not read this until you have read the previous page!)

Murder by poison! From memory, can you tell what changed between this and the previous page to pinpoint what was used as a weapon?

Cryptograms are messages in substitution code. For example, THE SMART CAT might become FVO QWGDF JGF if F is substituted for **T**, **V** for **H**, **O** for **E**, and so on. Break the code to reveal a quotation from a Sherlock Holmes adventure.

P ASNO FOJBPGJOX ZGFOTAOEO PJ

BAOZO PJVGAOEOJB FOFGPEZ, BAO

GHBQHEZBZ GL KSZZPGJSBO OJO-

EWU TAOJ AO KOELGEFOX BAO EOF-

SEMSQYO LOSBZ TPBA TAPVA APZ

JSFO PZ SZZGVPSBOX TOEO LGYYG-

TOX QU EOSVBPGJZ GL YOBASEWU

XHEPJW TAPVA AO TGHYX YPO

SQGHB TPBA APZ NPGYPJ SJX APZ

QGGMZ, ASEXYU FGNPJW ZSNO

LEGF BAO ZGLS BG BAO BSQYO.

– BAO FHZWESNO EPBHSY

67

Answers on page 179.

Interception

Sherlock Holmes intercepted a message that is meant to reveal a location for an upcoming meeting between two criminal masterminds. The only problem is, the message shows many place names. Can you figure out the right location?

MINSK

CAIRO

DELHI

KABUL

ABUJA

VADUZ

Stormy Night

Below is a quotation from a Sherlock Holmes story. Rearrange each set of scrambled capital letters to reveal the missing word. Bonus: Name the Sherlock Holmes adventure from which this quotation is drawn.

It was a wild, SMEPUUTETOS _____ night, towards the close of

OVENBMRE _____. Holmes and I sat together in NSILEEC _____

all the evening, he engaged with a powerful lens ECGRPIDNIHE

_____ the remains of the original TSIRCNIIONP _____ upon a

SPEAMLIPST _____, I deep in a recent TSATEIRE _____ upon

YURGRES _____. Outside the wind howled down Baker Street, while

the rain beat fiercely against the windows. It was RTGSEAN _____

there, in the very depths of the town, with ten miles of man's RADIKNHOW

_____ on every side of us, to feel the iron grip of ATNRUE _____, and

to be conscious that to the huge ALMLNTEEE _____ forces all London

was no more than the IMHLOSLLE _____ that dot the fields.

Answers on page 180.

1. Moriarty is a professor of what?

   A. Criminology

   B. History

   C. Mathematics

   D. Chemistry

2. Where do Holmes and Moriarty meet for their final confrontation?

   A. 221b Baker Street

   B. St. Bartholomew's Hospital

   C. Baskerville Hall

   D. Reichenbach Falls

3. How long is Holmes missing after confronting Moriarty?

   A. 1 year

   B. 3 years

   C. 10 years

   D. 7 months

4. Moriarty is likely based on which real criminal?

   A. Jack the Ripper

   B. Adam Worth

   C. Richard Dadd

   D. William Henry Bury

Answers on page 180.

Read the story below, then turn the page and answer the questions.

While on a train, a bystander overheard a conversation where one person was giving another the passwords for a set of underground gambling clubs. The bystander heard that the password for the south side club was, "My friend Leonardo swears by this place." At the north side location, the password was, "My friend Ritchie might be working the kitchens, do you know if he's on tonight?" At the Main Street location, the password is, "My friend James said your fish was the best." At the riverfront location, the password is, "My friend Harold said the burgers here would make the angels weep." At the suburban location, the password is, "Is Janey the chef tonight?"

Overheard Information (Part II)

(Do not read this until you have read the previous page!)

1. The password for the riverfront location is: "My friend Harold said the burgers here would make the angels weep."

    _____ True

    _____ False

2. The password for the north side location is: "My friend James said your fish was the best."

    _____ True

    _____ False

3. The password for the south side location is: "My friend Leonardo might be working the kitchens, do you know if he's on tonight?"

    _____ True

    _____ False

4. The password for the suburban location is: "Is Janey the chef tonight?"

    _____ True

    _____ False

Answers on page 180.

A Convincing Facade

Cryptograms are messages in substitution code. For example, THE SMART CAT might become FVO QWGDF JGF if F is substituted for T, V for H, O for E, and so on. Break the code to read the quote fro a Sherlock Holmes adventure. Bonus: Name the story from which the quote was drawn.

TX S QEVQYQP, S XTL, SV SX VYWQ, TE WELDEVQP VSPSEQXX,

ZWV VJQ DMP MTEPHTYIX LQYQ TMM SE VJQSY FMTGQ. VJQYQ

LQYQ VJQ GJQHSGTM GDYEQY TEP VJQ TGSP-XVTSEQP, PQTM-

VDFFQP VTZMQ. VJQYQ WFDE T XJQMO LTX VJQ YDL DO

ODYHSPTZMQ XGYTFZDDIX TEP ZDDIX DO YQOQYQEGQ LJSGJ

HTEU DO DWY OQMMDL GSVSNQEX LDWMP JTCQ ZQQE XD RMTP

VD ZWYE. VJQ PSTRYTHX, VJQ CSDMSE-GTXQ, TEP VJQ FSFQ-

YTGI—QCQE VJQ FQYXSTE XMSFFQY LJSGJ GDEVTSEQP VJQ

VDZTGGD—TMM HQV HU QUQX TX S RMTEGQP YDWEP HQ. VJQYQ

LQYQ VLD DGGWFTEVX DO VJQ YDDH—DEQ, HYX. JWPXDE, LJD

ZQTHQP WFDE WX ZDVJ TX LQ QEVQYQP—VJQ DVJQY, VJQ

XVYTERQ PWHHU LJSGJ JTP FMTUQP XD SHFDYVTEV T FTYV SE

VJQ QCQESER'X TPCQEVWYQX. SV LTX T LTK-GDMDYQP HDPQM

DO HU OYSQEP, XD TPHSYTZMU PDEQ VJTV SV LTX T FQYOQGV

OTGXSHSMQ. SV XVDDP DE T XHTMM FQPQXVTM VTZMQ LSVJ TE

DMP PYQXXSER-RDLE DO JDMHQX'X XD PYTFQP YDWEP SV VJTV

VJQ SMMWXSDE OYDH VJQ XVYQQV LTX TZXDMWVQMU FQYOQGV.

73

Answers on page 180.

Match each Sherlock Holmes short story with the book in which it appears.

1. The Adventure of the Silver Blaze

A. The Return of Sherlock Holmes

2. The Adventure of the Dancing Men

B. His Last Bow

C. The Case-Book of Sherlock Holmes

3. The Adventure of the Bruce-Partington Plans

D. The Memoirs of Sherlock Holmes

4. The Adventure of the Veiled Lodger

Answers on page 180.

Domestic Logic

On Box Street, there are 5 adjacent houses that are identical to each other. You've been asked to visit Mr. Jones, but without any addresses on the doors you are not sure which house to approach. At the local coffee shop, you ask the waitress for help. She is able to provide the following information:

A. Mr. Jones has 2 neighbors.

B. The house in the middle is occupied by an elderly woman.

C. Mary lives between the elderly woman and a family of 3 children.

D. The 3 children live in House A.

Can you determine which is Mr. Jones's house?

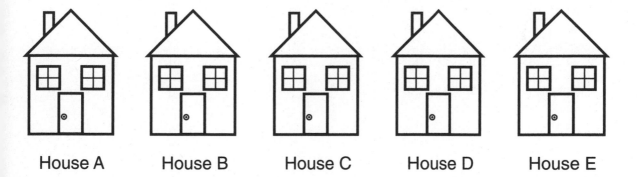

House A　　House B　　House C　　House D　　House E

Answers on page 180.

Across the Moors

Every word or phrase in all capital letters is contained within the group of letters. Words can be found in a straight line horizontally, vertically, or diagonally. They may be read either forward or backward.

On the land side, our SURROUNDINGS were as SOMBER as on the sea. It was a COUNTRY of rolling MOORS, lonely and DUN-COLORED, with an occasional CHURCH tower to mark the site of some OLD-WORLD village. In every DIRECTION upon these moors there were TRACES of some VANISHED race which had passed UTTERLY away and left as its sole RECORD strange MONUMENTS of stone, irregular MOUNDS which contained the BURNED ashes of the DEAD, and curious EARTHWORKS which hinted at PREHISTORIC strife. The GLAMOR and MYSTERY of the place, with its SINISTER atmosphere of FORGOTTEN nations, appealed to the IMAGINATION of my friend, and he spent much of his time in long WALKS and solitary MEDITATIONS upon the moor.

– The Adventure of the Devil's Foot

```
Y N R A U H S X V K F Y C N D O K H
M B D W J C O J A A R C E X L E Y P
G U R M O U N D S E N T K D T R A Y
F R O S N S A G T K T I W Z T Q L D
X N C R Z Y O S L O C O S N M R G X
M E E O P V Y M G A R A U H E V V M
S D R O R M E R B L M O A T E W H L
U Q S M E S O A D E C O T A Q D O Z
R F N S H F T Y D S R U R Q H I K Y
R T O S I Y A N F E R E T S I N I S
O R I J S M B P E M R Z C A X L W P
U A T Z T K O Y L M V O O H L M A O
N C A F O Z C X G L U S L D B H L M
D E T D R L I Y A P S N O O F E K N
I S I D I R E C T I O N O S C Y S L
N T D P C I H C R U H C F M M N R Q
G U E A R T H W O R K S N I W F U C
S E M Z K N O I T A N I G A M I F D
```

77

Answers on page 181.

Below is a group of words that, when properly arranged in the blanks, reveal a quote from the Sherlock Holmes adventure "The Five Orange Pips."

BLEND

DEEP

FINE

GALE

HOWL

LENGTHEN

SPLASH

SWASH

I...was _____ in one of Clark

Russell's _____ sea-stories,

until the _____ of the _____

from without seemed to _____

with the text, and the _____ of

the rain to _____ out into the

long _____ of the sea waves.

Answers on page 181.

Read the story below, then turn the page and answer the questions.

Sherlock Holmes overheard the thief tell her accomplice about the different places where she stashed the loot. She said, "I left the largest diamond taped to the drainpipe underneath the upstairs sink. The four smaller diamonds are tucked in a pair of pantyhose in the third drawer down in the dresser. The gold necklace is wrapped up in the rose-patterned pillowcase in the linen closet. The gold bars are in a locked trunk in the attic."

(Do not read this until you have read the previous page!)

Holmes overheard the information about where the stolen loot was stored, but didn't have anywhere to write it down! Answer the questions below to help him remember.

1. What is found in the drainpipe?

   A. The largest diamond

   B. The four smaller diamonds

   C. The gold necklace

   D. The pearl

2. The gold necklace is wrapped in this.

   A. Pantyhose

   B. Plain pillowcase

   C. Rose-patterned pillowcase

   D. Sock

3. The gold bars are in this.

   A. The linen closet

   B. A locked trunk in the attic

   C. A trunk in the crawlspace

   D. A trunk in the basement

4. Which item or items are found in the top dresser drawer?

   A. The largest diamond

   B. The four smaller diamonds

   C. The gold necklace

   D. None of them

Answers on page 181.

Annoying Mystery

Below is a quotation from a Sherlock Holmes story. Rearrange each set of scrambled capital letters to reveal the missing word. Bonus: Name the Sherlock Holmes adventure from which this quotation is drawn.

All that day and the next and the next Holmes was in a mood which his friends would call TTARUCIN _____, and others EORMSO _____. He ran out and ran in, smoked ETYNLISCASN _____, played snatches on his violin, sank into EESVRIRE _____, devoured SHICNSEDAW _____ at irregular hours, and hardly answered the ALUASC _____ questions which I put to him. It was evident to me that things were not going well with him or his quest. He would say nothing of the case, and it was from the ESPAPR _____ that I learned the PTUACRSAIRL _____ of the EUTSNQI _____, and the arrest with the SUTUNEEBSQ _____ release of John Mitton, the valet of the ESEDAECD _____. The coroner's jury brought in the SOOVIBU _____ Willful Murder, but the TPEASRI _____ remained as un-known as ever.

Answers on page 181.

Crime...and Logic

Cryptograms are messages in substitution code. Break the code to read the message. For example, THE SMART CAT might become FVO QWGDF JGF if **F** is substituted for **T**, **V** for **H**, **O** for **E**, and so on.

PJKLB KO PQLLQH. ZQSKP KO JUJB.

NABJBEQJB KN KO TDQH NAB ZQSKP

JUNABJ NAUH TDQH NAB PJKLB

NAUN RQT OAQTZC CFBZZ.

Answers on page 181.

Where It Happened

Match each event in Sherlock Holmes' adventures with the place in which it occurs.

1. Where Watson served in the military

2. Where Holmes finally confronted Moriarty

3. Location of Baskerville Hall

4. Irene Adler's birthplace

A. Afghanistan

B. New Jersey

C. Switzerland

D. Scotland

83

Answers on page 181.

Coded Note

Sherlock Holmes found a list from the burglar and thinks it might indicate what the burglar plans to steal. But in addition to being scrambled, each word or phrase below is missing the same letter. Discover the missing letter, then unscramble the words. When you do, you'll find out what the burglar's targets are.

MAD NODS

A RAT

ADD ME

FINE RUG

Answers on page 182.

Sherlock Holmes learned the information below while trying to solve a mystery. Read the text, then turn the page for a quiz on what you've read.

Mr. Lucas is an unmarried man, thirty-four years of age, and his establishment consists of Mrs. Pringle, an elderly housekeeper, and of Mitton, his valet. The former retires early and sleeps at the top of the house. The valet was out for the evening, visiting a friend at Hammersmith. From ten o'clock onward Mr. Lucas had the house to himself. What occurred during that time has not yet transpired, but at a quarter to twelve Police-constable Barrett, passing along Godolphin Street observed that the door of No. 16 was ajar. He knocked, but received no answer. Perceiving a light in the front room, he advanced into the passage and again knocked, but without reply. He then pushed open the door and entered. The room was in a state of wild disorder, the furniture being all swept to one side, and one chair lying on its back in the center. Beside this chair, and still grasping one of its legs, lay the unfortunate tenant of the house. He had been stabbed to the heart and must have died instantly. The knife with which the crime had been committed was a curved Indian dagger, plucked down from a trophy of Oriental arms which adorned one of the walls.

The Adventure of the Second Stain
(Part II)

(Do not read this until you have read the previous page!)

1. How old was Mr. Lucas?

   A. 25

   B. 34

   C. 44

   D. 56

2. At what time did Police-constable Barrett pass by the house?

   A. Quarter to twelve

   B. Half past eleven

   C. Ten til one

   D. One o'clock

3. How many times did Barrett stop to knock on a door before finding Mr. Lucas?

   A. Once

   B. Twice

   C. Three times

   D. He did not knock

4. What weapon was used against Mr. Lucas?

   A. Pistol

   B. Sword

   C. Kitchen knife

   D. Dagger

Answers on page 182.

Below is a quotation from a Sherlock Holmes story. Rearrange each set of scrambled capital letters to reveal the missing word. Bonus: Name the Sherlock Holmes adventure from which this quotation is drawn.

I must admit, Watson, that you have some power of SNICETEOL

_____, which ETSNAO _____ for much which I ELRPEOD

_____ in your TNISERRVAA _____. Your FTAAL _____ habit

of looking at everything from the point of view of a story instead of as a

IIESNFCCIT _____ exercise has ruined what might have been an

UEITCINSTVR _____ and even ALSCCSAIL _____ series of

SINDMERTSOANTO _____. You RLSU _____ over work of the

utmost ESFEINS _____ and LDCYIACE _____, in order to dwell

upon ONSISATLNAE _____ details which may excite, but cannot pos-

sibly instruct, the reader.

Answers on page 182.

1. What was Watson's job before meeting Holmes?

    A. Army surgeon

    B. Private doctor

    C. Naval officer

    D. Medical student

2. What does Watson refer to when he mentions "battle signals" in The Adventure of the Gold Pince-Nez?

    A. The sound of Holmes playing violin

    B. Holmes shouting, "That's it!"

    C. Holmes' shining eyes and colored cheeks

    D. The sirens of police vehicles

3. In what Conan Doyle-written adventure do we see Watson and Holmes celebrating Christmas?

    A. The Christmas Demon

    B. The Hound of the Baskervilles

    C. The Five Orange Pips

    D. The Adventure of the Blue Carbuncle

4. What year do Watson and Holmes first meet?

    A. 1881

    B. 1889

    C. 1901

    D. 1912

Answers on page 182.

Fingerprint Match

Find the matching fingerprint(s). There may be more than one.

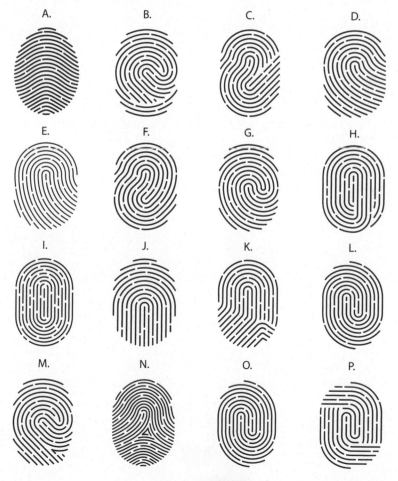

A.   B.   C.   D.

E.   F.   G.   H.

I.   J.   K.   L.

M.   N.   O.   P.

Answers on page 182.

Mrs. Hudson

Below is a quotation from a Sherlock Holmes adventure. Every word or phrase in all capital letters is contained within the group of letters. Words can be found in a straight line horizontally, vertically, or diagonally. They may be read either forward or backward.

Mrs. HUDSON, the LANDLADY of Sherlock Holmes, was a LONG-SUFFERING woman. Not only was her first-floor flat INVADED at all hours by THRONGS of SINGULAR and often UNDESIRABLE characters but her remarkable LODGER showed an ECCENTRICITY and IRREGULARITY in his life which must have sorely tried her PATIENCE. His incredible UNTIDINESS, his ADDICTION to music at STRANGE hours, his occasional REVOLVER practice within doors, his WEIRD and often MALODOROUS scientific EXPERIMENTS, and the ATMOSPHERE of VIOLENCE and DANGER which hung around him made him the very WORST tenant in LONDON.

– The Adventure of the Dying Detective

```
R W C Y T I C I R T N E C C E Z H Y
V U G V W E E M Q R E V L O V E R L
I I N N M O R B S T R A N G E U O V
X V O T I X R E S W E I R D I N S M
H K D L I R I S H Z U B L R D D W U
V O V R E D E C T P D G R O P E G E
A I Z E G N I F E E S E N L Q S R Q
M A Y G L A C N F C G O X N N I A E
A B D D N Z D E E U M L M N J R L O
L X A O P F K D L S S R U T U A U A
O G L L H T A A I V S G F F A B G I
D Z D H X U R W Y C T R N S I L N N
O A N U K I D G K C T H E O Y E I V
R B A P T V P S E J X I R G L E S A
O X L Y I L S M O I G I O O N L H D
U E X P E R I M E N T S D N N A O E
S N E L P A T I E N C E M S U G D D
I X C T W S Y I B L W Y D T J T S N
```

Answers on page 182.

Motel Hideout

A thief hides out in one of the 45 motel rooms listed in the chart below. Sherlock Holmes received a sheet of four clues, signed "The Logical Thief." Using these clues, the detective found the room number within 15 minutes—but by that time, the thief had fled. Can you find the thief's motel room quicker?

1. Multiply the first digit by 2 to get the second digit.

2. The first digit is a prime number.

3. The second digit is not prime.

4. It is not divisible by 9.

51	52	53	54	55	56	57	58	59
41	42	43	44	45	46	47	48	49
31	32	33	34	35	36	37	38	39
21	22	23	24	25	26	27	28	29
11	12	13	14	15	16	17	18	19

Answers on page 183.

The Adventure of the Empty House (Part I)

Sherlock Holmes learned the information below while trying to solve a mystery. Read the text, then turn the page for a quiz on what you've read.

On the evening of the crime, Ronald Adair returned from the club exactly at ten. His mother and sister were out spending the evening with a relation. The servant deposed that she heard him enter the front room on the second floor, generally used as his sitting-room. She had lit a fire there, and as it smoked she had opened the window. No sound was heard from the room until eleven-twenty, the hour of the return of Lady Maynooth and her daughter. Desiring to say goodnight, she attempted to enter her son's room. The door was locked on the inside, and no answer could be got to their cries and knocking. Help was obtained, and the door forced. The unfortunate young man was found lying near the table. His head had been horribly mutilated by an expanding revolver bullet, but no weapon of any sort was to be found in the room.

(Do not read this until you have read the previous page!)

1. Why did the servant open a window?

   A. The fire smoked

   B. It was too hot

   C. There was a sound outside

   D. The room smelled stale

2. When did Ronald Adair return from the club?

   A. At 8:00

   B. At 10:00

   C. At 11:20

   D. At midnight

3. For what did Roger Adair use the front room on the second floor?

   A. A bedroom

   B. A dressing room

   C. A storage room

   D. A sitting room

4. Who was Ronald Adair to Lady May-nooth?

   A. Her nephew

   B. Her brother

   C. Her cousin

   D. Her son

Answers on page 183.

Cryptograms are messages in substitution code. For example, THE SMART CAT might become FVO QWGDF JGF if **F** is substituted for **T**, **V** for **H**, **O** for **E**, and so on. Break the code to reveal a quotation from a Sherlock Holmes adventure.

NO BX HNO APGKDOKA KI WTBRO,

YPHXKA. NO BX HNO KTUPABMOT KI

NPDI HNPH BX OZBD PAE KI AOPTDF

PDD HNPH BX QAEOHOWHOE BA HNBX

UTOPH WBHF. NO BX P UOABQX, P

GNBDKXKGNOT, PA PLXHTPWH HNBA-

COT. NO NPX P LTPBA KI HNO IBTXH

KTEOT. NO XBHX RKHBKADOXX, DBCO P

XGBEOT BA HNO WOAHOT KI BHX YOL,

LQH HNPH YOL NPX P HNKQXPAE TPEB-

PHBKAX, PAE NO CAKYX YODD OZOTF

JQBZOT KI OPWN KI HNOR.

– HNO IBAPD GTKLDOR

95

Answers on page 183.

On Riverdell Street, there are 5 houses. You need to follow up with a witness, Harriet Chin, but without any address on the doors you are not sure which house to approach. You know from the previous interview that Chin is a single mother with a daughter. The staff at the corner bakery and your own observations give you some clues. From the information given, can you find the right house?

A. The two corner houses are green, while the others are blue. There is a child or children living in one green house and two blue houses.

B. An elderly widower lives alone in the middle house.

C. The nanny for the couple in house E regularly brings her charge by for a treat at the bakery.

D. Sometimes she brings in the daughter of her next door neighbor, but the nanny doesn't like the boy further down the street.

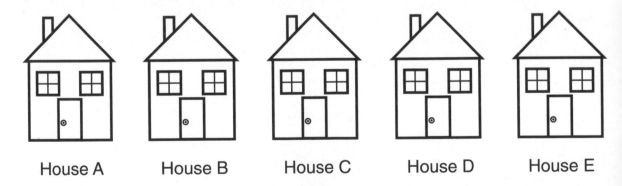

House A   House B   House C   House D   House E

Answers on page 183.

Country Vicar

Below is a quotation from a Sherlock Holmes story. Rearrange each set of scrambled capital letters to reveal the missing word. Bonus: Name the Sherlock Holmes adventure from which this quotation is drawn.

I have said that ECRDSTETA _____ towers marked the ALLEIVGS _____ which DEDTTO _____ this part of Cornwall. The ETNEARS _____ of these was the LEMTHA _____ of Tredannick Wollas, where the cottages of a couple of hundred inhabitants clustered round an NCEATNI _____, moss-grown church. The vicar of the parish, Mr. Roundhay, was something of an HTCLOSAGROIE _____, and as such Holmes had made his CAIEUNQATACN _____. He was a middle-aged man, PTOYRL _____ and BFLEAAF _____, with a SENDRLCABIOE _____ fund of local lore. At his invitation we had taken tea at the AGARCEIV _____ and had come to know, also, Mr. Mortimer Tregennis, an ENNENPTDEID _____ gentleman, who IENAECDSR _____ the clergyman's scanty SRUERCSOE _____ by taking rooms in his large, NGRTLAGGIS _____ house.

Answers on page 183.

Below is a quotation from a Sherlock Holmes adventure. Every word or phrase in all capital letters is contained within the group of letters. Words can be found in a straight line horizontally, vertically, or diagonally. They may be read either forward or backward.

This BARRICADED door CORRESPONDED clearly with the SHUTTERED window outside, and yet I could see by the GLIMMER from beneath it that the room was not in DARKNESS. Evidently there was a SKYLIGHT which let in light from ABOVE. As I stood in the PASSAGE gazing at the SINISTER door and wondering what SECRET it might VEIL, I suddenly heard the SOUND of steps within the room and saw a SHADOW pass BACKWARD and FORWARD against the little SLIT of dim light which SHONE out from under the door. A mad, unreasoning TERROR rose up in me at the sight, Mr. Holmes. My OVERSTRUNG nerves FAILED me suddenly, and I TURNED and ran—ran as though some DREADFUL hand were BEHIND me CLUTCHING at the SKIRT of my dress.

– The Adventure of the Copper Beeches

```
N L B A C K W A R D T E Q K G F Z G
V C U U S U U R Z F D H E J C S J N
D D D F M E E G I L A U G Q C H Y B
H D R T D M C W T C J I T I L S A X
Z D H A M A A R O Z P G L S L R V F
S X C I W B E C E D C N H E R Y A X
I Z L O O R S R C T A O B I D E K S
N G G V K S O H D E N H C Y G D S S
I B E D E G T F U E M A S B U N S G
S M T E R R O R B T D J Z C D U E N
T D P N V P O M C E T E Z F D O N I
E K U R N P O B D J S E V J L S K H
R U B U P A S S A G E U R Z T D R C
K L M T U D W T T G Q C A E X N A T
V G N U R T S R E V O K C L D I D U
C O R R E S P O N D E D I S Q H U L
V Y Z T R I K S G Y V E C A R E Z C
V E Z O Q H X P D E V T U N F B K L
```

99

Answers on page 183.

They Played Sherlock

ACROSS

1. ___ Rathbone played Sherlock on radio, stage, TV, and film, 1939–53
6. Floating among the clouds
11. "All ___, by the telephone..."
12. One of the simple machines
13. Bitten by a bug
14. Café quaff in Paris
15. Gallic seasoning
16. Holiday threshold
18. $200 Monopoly properties, briefly
19. He played Sherlock on 1938 radio (CBS)
22. Lumber pieces: abbr.
23. Wing, in Paris
24. Apple centers
27. Combats of honor
28. Edgar Rice Burroughs animals
29. Preposition in many Grafton titles
30. He played Sherlock on 1983 animated TV (Australian)
35. Joseph Lincoln book "Cap'n ___"
36. "___ Haw" (rustic TV show)
37. Backside, in French
38. Like the worm-catching bird
40. Kitchen chopper
42. Engine power source

43. Grown-up
44. "Siddhartha" author Hermann
45. Leonard ___ played Sherlock on stage (Royal Shakespeare Company, 1976)

DOWN

1. Deep voice at the opera
2. Put on cuffs, maybe
3. Spiritual essences
4. Homey lodging
5. Tall tales of yore
6. "A Zoo Story" playwright Edward
7. "Hawaii Five-O" prop
8. Blanket
9. Will ___ played Sherlock on film ("Holmes and Watson," 2018)
10. Locks without keys
17. Beetles and Rabbits, for short
20. Beyond chubby
21. Achille ___: hijacked liner
24. Facetious "Get it?"
25. Run, as heavy machinery
26. Stops working
27. Spoiled rotten, maybe
29. Any Hatfield, to a McCoy
31. Squeegee for Luigi, e.g.
32. Creator of a logical "razor"
33. "Hasta ___" ("Goodbye")

34. Kingly title in Spain

39. Word with Cruces or Palmas

41. "___ Ran the Zoo" (Dr. Seuss book)

1	2	3	4	5		6	7	8	9	10
11						12				
13						14				
15				16	17			18		
19			20			21				
			22			23				
24	25	26				27				
28					29					
30				31				32	33	34
35				36				37		
38			39			40	41			
42						43				
44						45				

101

Answers on page 184.

Say What?

Below is a group of words that, when properly arranged in the blanks, reveal a quote from the Sherlock Holmes adventure "The Five Orange Pips."

CHAIN

DEDUCE

EVENTS

FOLLOW

IDEAL

RESULTS

SHOWN

SINGLE

"The _____ reasoner," [Holmes] remarked, "would, when he had once been _____ a _____ fact in all its bearings, _____ from it not only all the _____ of _____ which led up to it, but also all the _____ which would _____ from it."

Answers on page 184.

The Murderous Gem Thief

5 types of gems were stolen from the murder scene. There was 1 gem of the first type, 2 of the second type, 3 of the third type, 4 of the fourth type, and 5 of the fifth type. From the information given below, can you tell how many gemstones of each kind were taken?

1. There are twice as many pearls as diamonds, but fewer pearls than pieces of jade.

2. Rubies are not the rarest gem.

3. There are an even number of sapphires.

4. Rubies are not the most plentiful gem.

Answers on page 184.

Patience

Below is a quotation from a Sherlock Holmes adventure. Every word or phrase in all capital letters is contained within the group of letters. Words can be found in a straight line horizontally, vertically, or diagonally. They may be read either forward or backward.

One of the most REMARKABLE characteristics of SHERLOCK Holmes was his POWER of THROWING his BRAIN out of action and SWITCHING all his THOUGHTS on to LIGHTER things whenever he had CONVINCED himself that he could no longer work to ADVANTAGE. I remember that during the whole of that MEMORABLE day he lost himself in a MONOGRAPH which he had UNDERTAKEN upon the POLYPHONIC Motets of Lassus. For my own part I had none of this power of DETACHMENT, and the day, in CONSEQUENCE, appeared to be INTERMINABLE. The great NATIONAL importance of the issue, the SUSPENSE in high QUARTERS, the direct nature of the EXPERIMENT which we were trying—all combined to work upon my NERVE. It was a RELIEF to me when at last, after a LIGHT dinner, we set out upon our EXPEDITION.

– The Adventure of the Bruce-Partington Plans

```
J D K M D R I U D D E C N I V N O C
X G X H E X R V U B T H G I L U X N
N N A I R M J R Q M Y N E R E O O Z
E I U W O F O A E O G S W C K I T H
K H W V I T R H M N A N F T B H L
A C I J J K Q P A E A E I I C L O A
T T D N D E A C P B U R D Q A M U N
R I Q U T R O S I Q L E K D G Z G O
E W F T G E U G E N P E V A Y B H I
D S W O Q S R S N X O U P R B K T T
N B N Y R H N M E I S H M O E L S A
U O H J F O X K I L W H P J W N E N
M Z X B C J Z O C N B O E Y N E D I
A D V A N T A G E G A A R R L W R A
R E T H G I L M O H G B Q H L O M R
E X P E R I M E N T Y B L A T O P B
T N E M H C A T E D D K H E T V C N
S R E L I E F F F S R E T R A U Q K
```

105

Answers on page 184.

You've intercepted a message. You think it might be the location of a meeting between two criminals, but it doesn't seem to make sense. Can you decipher the true message?

WILL SKIING HUBBLE BURR BAA URR YAY

IMMUNE SOON INNS MEDDLE AARDWOLF

YUCKY

Sherlock Holmes learned the information below while trying to solve a mystery. Read the text, then turn the page for a quiz on what you've read.

"You must surely remember the great Worthingdon bank business," said Holmes. "Five men were in it—these four and a fifth called Cartwright. Tobin, the caretaker, was murdered, and the thieves got away with seven thousand pounds. This was in 1875. They were all five arrested, but the evidence against them was by no means conclusive. This Blessington or Sutton, who was the worst of the gang, turned informer. On his evidence, Cartwright was hanged and the other three got fifteen years apiece. When they got out the other day, which was some years before their full term, they set themselves, as you perceive, to hunt down the traitor and to avenge the death of their comrade upon him. Twice they tried to get at him and failed; a third time, you see, it came off."

(Do not read this until you have read the previous page!)

1. What was the name of the murdered caretaker?

    A. Cartwright

    B. Worthingdon

    C. Tobin

    D. Sutton

2. How much did the thieves initially get away with in 1875?

    A. 3 thousand pounds

    B. 7 thousand pounds

    C. 10 thousand pounds

    D. 20 thousand pounds

3. What was the sentence for three members of the gang in response for the theft?

    A. 15 years

    B. 20 years

    C. Life

    D. Hanging

4. How many attempts did it take for the gang to "get at" the informer?

    A. 2 attempts

    B. 3 attempts

    C. 5 attempts

    D. They never succeeded

Answers on page 184.

Pick Your Poison

There are four bottles before you, but they've gotten jumbled up. Poison is found in one of them. If you arrange them from left to right, following the instructions given below, you will be able to know where the poison is found.

1. The bottles are red, yellow, green, and purple, but not necessarily in that order.

2. The second bottle from the left is the largest bottle. The smallest bottle is not right next to it.

3. The poison is not found in the smallest bottle.

4. The poison is not found in the bottle of a primary color.

5. The yellow bottle is the largest, while the green is the smallest.

6. The red bottle is not found on the end.

109

Answers on page 185.

Cryptograms are messages in substitution code. Break the code to reveal a quotation from a Sherlock Holmes story. For example, THE SMART CAT might become FVO QWGDF JGF if **F** is substituted for **T**, **V** for **H**, **O** for **E**, and so on. Bonus: Name the Sherlock Holmes adventure from which this quotation was drawn.

MZEFINHO ZNIGEM DYM, YM P EQAEHKEW, INLJXPJX

YBNLK ZPM MPKKPJX-FNNG PJ ZPM WFEMMPJX-XNDJ,

FEYWPJX KZE YXNJT HNILGJ NV KZE KPGEM YJW

MGNOPJX ZPM BEVNFE-BFEYOVYMK APAE, DZPHZ

DYM HNGANMEW NV YII KZE AILXM YJW WNKKIEM

IEVK VFNG ZPM MGNOEM NV KZE WYT BEVNFE, YII

HYFEVLIIT WFPEW YJW HNIIEHKEW NJ KZE HNFJEF

NV KZE GYJKEIAPEHE. ZE FEHEPCEW LM PJ ZPM

SLPEKIT XEJPYI VYMZPNJ, NFWEFEW VFEMZ

FYMZEFM YJW EXXM, YJW RNPJEW LM PJ Y ZEYFKT

GEYI. DZEJ PK DYM HNJHILWEW ZE MEKKIEW NLF

JED YHSLYPJKYJHE LANJ KZE MNVY, AIYHEW Y APIIND

BEJEYKZ ZPM ZEYW, YJW IYPW Y XIYMM NV BFYJWT

YJW DYKEF DPKZPJ ZPM FEYHZ.

Holmes Pop Quiz

1. What kind of hat does Holmes traditionally wear?

    A. Derby

    B. Ascot

    C. Deerstalker

    D. Homburg

2. Which Holmes adventure was the basis of a film reportedly found in Hitler's Bunker?

    A. The Valley of Fear

    B. The Blue Carbuncle

    C. A Scandal in Bohemia

    D. The Hound of the Baskervilles

3. What is Holmes' group of intelligence agents called?

    A. Baker Street Irregulars

    B. Homes' Boys

    C. Agents of Scotland Yard

    D. They didn't have a name

4. Who is part of this group of intelligence agents?

    A. Off-duty police officers

    B. Local boys on the street

    C. Government agents

    D. Mrs. Hudson

111

Answers on page 185.

Conan Doyle and Characters

Match each person with the year they were born.

1. Irene Adler

A. 1854

2. Sherlock Holmes

B. 1858

3. Arthur Conan Doyle

C. 1852

4. Dr. John Watson

D. 1859

Answers on page 185.

Overheard Information (Part I)

Read the story below, then turn the page and answer the questions.

Sherlock Holmes overheard the thief telling his accomplice where the stolen loot was stored— on 41 S. 6th Street, on the 4th floor, in the 2nd room on the left, in a safe with the combination 34-43-434.

Overheard Information (Part II)

(Do not read this until you have read the previous page!)

Holmes overheard the information about where the stolen loot was stored, but didn't have anywhere to write it down! Answer the questions below to help him remember.

1. What was the street address?
   - **A.** 41 N. 6th St.
   - **B.** 41 S. 6th St.
   - **C.** 6 N. 41st St.
   - **D.** 6 S. 41st St.

2. What floor?
   - **A.** 1st
   - **B.** 2nd
   - **C.** 3rd
   - **D.** 4th

3. Was the room on the left or the right side of the hallway?
   - **A.** Left
   - **B.** Right

4. What was the combination to the safe?
   - **A.** 43-34-434
   - **B.** 34-34-434
   - **C.** 34-43-434
   - **D.** 34-43-343

Answers on page 185.

On the Scene

Below is a quotation from a Sherlock Holmes story. Rearrange each set of scrambled capital letters to reveal the missing word. Bonus: Name the Sherlock Holmes adventure from which this quotation is drawn.

It was my first visit to the ESNEC _____ of the MREIC _____—a high, NGYID _____, narrow-chested SEUOH _____, prim, MRLFAO _____, and solid, like the RCEUNYT _____ which gave it birth. Lestrade's LBGDOUL _____ features gazed out at us from the front window, and he greeted us WYRMAL _____ when a big BLSNETOAC _____ had opened the door and let us in. The room into which we were shown was that in which the crime had been committed, but no trace of it now remained save an ugly, LURGAIRRE _____ stain upon the carpet. This carpet was a small UQREAS _____ drugget in the center of the room, surrounded by a DOBRA _____ expanse of IABLUEFTU _____, old-fashioned wood flooring in square blocks, highly polished. Over the RIFEAEPLC _____ was a GEFNITACNMI _____ trophy of WSAENPO _____, one of which had been used on that tragic night. In the window was a TOSUUUSMP _____ writing desk, and every detail of the NRTPMAEAT _____, the CRUITEPS _____, the rugs, and the INSNGAHG _____, all pointed to a taste which was UOLUXSRUI _____.

Answers on page 185.

Oops! Four mugshots accidentally got sent through the shredder, and Sherlock Holmes is trying to straighten them out. Currently, only one facial feature in each row is in its correct place. Holmes knows that:

1. C's nose is one place to the left of D's mouth.

2. C's eyes are one place to the right of C's hair.

3. B's nose is not next to C's nose.

4. A's eyes are 2 places to the left of A's mouth.

5. C's eyes are not next to A's eyes.

6. D's hair is one place to the right of B's nose.

Can you find the correct hair, eyes, nose, and mouth for each person?

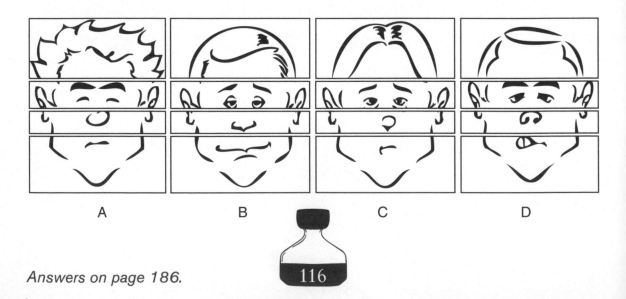

A   B   C   D

Answers on page 186.

Bank Mayhem

A criminal mastermind who calls himself "Trixter" has hidden a stolen artifact in one of forty-five different safety deposit boxes at the local bank. Each box has a different number, and the miscreant has given the police a series of clues that will point to its hidden location. Using only these clues, find the one correct number – but be careful! Open the wrong box and the priceless artifact will be destroyed.

1. It is odd.

2. It is divisible by a 2-digit prime number.

3. It is not divisible by 11.

4. It is not prime.

5. The sum of the digits is less than 10.

51	52	53	54	55	56	57	58	59
41	42	43	44	45	46	47	48	49
31	32	33	34	35	36	37	38	39
21	22	23	24	25	26	27	28	29
11	12	13	14	15	16	17	18	19

Answers on page 186.

Blue Carbuncle

Below is a quotation from a Sherlock Holmes adventure. Every word or phrase in all capital letters is contained within the group of letters. Words can be found in a straight line horizontally, vertically, or diagonally. They may be read either forward or backward.

Holmes took up the STONE and held it against the light. "It's a BONNY thing," said he. "Just see how it GLINTS and SPARKLES. Of course, it is a NUCLEUS and focus of CRIME. Every good stone is. They are the DEVIL'S pet BAITS. In the larger and older JEWELS every FACET may stand for a BLOODY deed. This stone is not yet TWENTY years old. It was found in the banks of the AMOY RIVER in southern CHINA and is remarkable in having every CHARACTERISTIC of the CARBUNCLE, save that it is BLUE in shade instead of RUBY RED. In spite of its youth, it has already a SINISTER history. There have been two MURDERS, a VITRIOL-THROWING, a suicide, and several ROBBERIES brought about for the sake of this FORTY-GRAIN weight of crystallized CHARCOAL."

— Adventure of the Blue Carbuncle

```
N M Y T N E W T U L R E P C F G G C
G O X D K M C V Z U M D H D L E A L
A C F E H U L X B I N A D P M R S B
M T L V U R P Y R X R B J A B Z L V
O H C I M D R C X A B J O U H U E G
Y H R L F E O D C V P A N N E L W F
R W P S D R R T Y F S C I E N J E A
I H W A J S E L K G L N W T T Y J C
V S T Z L R L K A E U D P N S D R E
E N G N I W O R H T L O I R T I V T
R B F S D K Q C H A R C O A L S L S
L D T K A F T V P L L W K H T F Z I
L I R F O R T Y G R A I N N A N D N
C S E I R E B B O R B X I L N E W I
X N U C L E U S H C N L V T I N L S
R A A B L O O D Y D G S K T H O M T
D J F F D G W Z O L N E A Z C T A E
P B U I J E S E L K R A P S P S C R
```

119

Answers on page 186.

Say What?

Below is a group of words that, when properly arranged in the blanks, reveal a quote from the Sherlock Holmes story "The Adventure of the Copper Beeches."

ADVERTISEMENT

ART

DERIVED

FREQUENTLY

IMPORTANT

LOWLIEST

MAN

PLEASURE

"To the _____ who loves _____ for its own sake," remarked Sherlock Holmes, tossing aside the _____ sheet of The Daily Telegraph, "it is _____ in its least _____ and _____ manifestations that the keenest _____ is to be _____."

Answers on page 186.

The Adventure of Charles Augustus Milverton

Choose the correct word or phrase to complete each quote from a Sherlock Holmes adventure.

1. The thick, warm air of the conservatory and the rich, choking fragrance of _____ plants took us by the throat.

    A. Blooming

    B. Exotic

    C. Strong-smelling

    D. Carniverous

2. He seized my hand in the darkness and led me swiftly past banks of _____ which brushed against our faces.

    A. Shrubs

    B. Coats

    C. Trees

    D. Flowers

3. [Holmes] opened a door, and I was vaguely conscious that we had entered a large room in which a _____ had been _____ not long before.

    A. Fire, lit

    B. Window, opened

    C. Letter, written

    D. Cigar, smoked

4. Something rushed out at us and my heart sprang into my mouth, but I could have _____ when I realized that it was the _____.

    A. Choked, burglar

    B. Bellowed, victim

    C. Laughed, cat

    D. Screamed, dog

Answers on page 186.

Domestic Logic

On Box Street, there are 5 adjacent houses that are identical to each other. You've been asked to visit Mr. Foreman, but without any addresses on the doors, you are not sure which house to approach. At the local coffee shop, you ask the waitress for help. She is able to provide the following information:

1. Two of the 5 houses contain children and adults.

2. Mr. Foreman lives alone.

3. Both houses with children have 2 neighboring properties and are not adjacent to each other.

4. The children often pass through Mrs. Cato's garden to play with each other.

5. The residents of the house located 2 spots to the right of Mrs. Cato's get along well with everyone on the street.

Which house does Mr. Foreman live in?

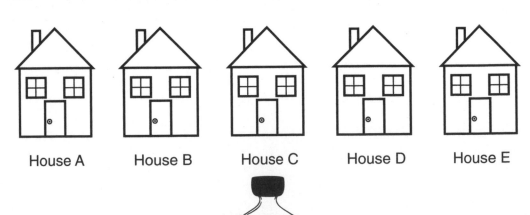

House A   House B   House C   House D   House E

Answers on page 186.

A Hidden Cache

Below is a quotation from a Sherlock Holmes story. Rearrange each set of scrambled capital letters to reveal the missing word. Bonus: Name the Sherlock Holmes adventure from which this quotation is drawn.

It was a small tin CBAXHSO _____ which stood upon the writing

desk. Holmes IRPDE _____ it open with his HCILSE _____.

Several rolls of paper were within, covered with ERSUFIG _____

and LALCUOATICSN _____, without any note to show to what

they referred. The RNGCIRUER _____ words, "water REPSUERS

_____" and "URRSEEPS _____ to the square inch" suggested

some possible INLRTEOA _____ to a IESMURABN _____. Holmes

SDESTO _____ them all ITPITYALENM _____ aside. There only

remained an VEEPOELN _____ with some small WNPEPSAER

_____ slips inside it.

Answers on page 187.

7 types of gems were stolen from the murder scene. There was 1 gem of the first type, 2 of the second type, 3 of the third type, 4 of the fourth type, 5 of the fifth type, 6 of the sixth type, and 7 of the seventh type. From the information given below, can you tell how many gemstones of each kind were taken?

1. There are fewer than 3 pieces of jade.

2. Diamonds are neither the most plentiful nor least plentiful gem.

3. There are an even number of topazes and an odd number of aquamarines.

4. There are twice as many rubies as sapphires, but not as many rubies as emeralds.

5. There are 3 more topazes than aquamarines.

6. There are more sapphires than aquamarines.

Study this picture for one minute, then turn the page.

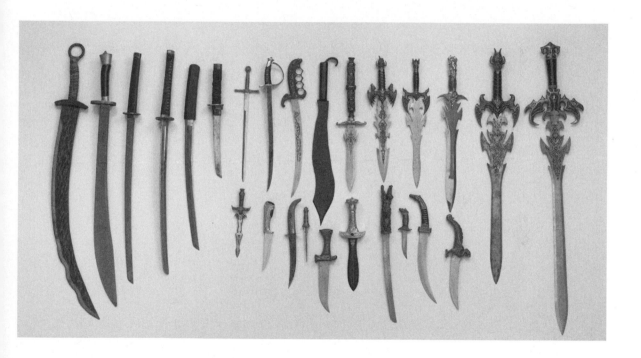

What Changed? (Part II)

(Do not read this until you have read the previous page!)

Murder by stabbing! From memory, can you tell what changed between this and the previous page to pinpoint what was used as a weapon?

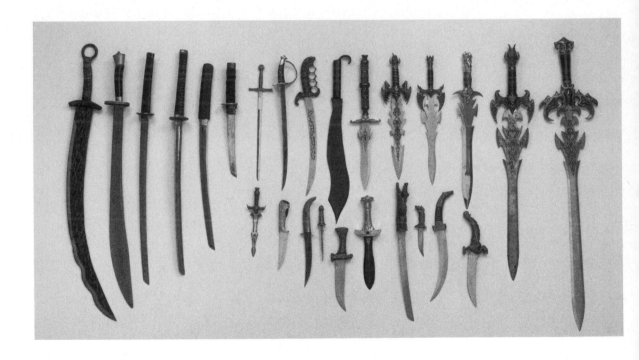

Cleaning Up

Cryptograms are messages in substitution code. For example, THE SMART CAT might become FVO QWGDF JGF if **F** is substituted for **T**, **V** for **H**, **O** for **E**, and so on. Bonus: Name the Sherlock Holmes adventure from which this quotation is drawn.

BZO UHZMOD'J ZHRGM, VJ UO JVM MBROMGOD CE
MGO IHDO, H XOZMKDOW MB JKRROJM MB GHS
MGVM, VJ GO GVW IHZHJGOW YVJMHZR ONMD-
VPMJ HZMB GHJ PBSSBZ-YQVPO CBBA, GO SHRGM
OSYQBE MGO ZONM MUB GBKDJ HZ SVAHZR BKD
DBBS V QHMMQO SBDO GVCHMVCQO. GO PBKQW
ZBM WOZE MGO FKJMHPO BI SE DOTKOJM, JB
UHMG V DVMGOD DKOIKQ IVPO GO UOZM BII MB
GHJ COWDBBS, IDBS UGHPG GO DOMKDZOW
YDOJOZMQE YKQQHZR V QVDRO MHZ CBN
COGHZW GHS. MGHJ GO YQVPOW HZ MGO
SHWWQO BI MGO IQBBD VZW, JTKVMMHZR WBUZ
KYBZ V JMBBQ HZ IDBZM BI HM, GO MGDOU CVPA
MGO QHW. H PBKQW JOO MGVM HM UVJ VQDOVWE
V MGHDW IKQQ BI CKZWQOJ BI YVYOD MHOW KY
UHMG DOW MVYO HZMB JOYVDVMO YVPAVROJ.

127

Answers on page 187.

Treasure Hunt

The treasure hunter visited eight cities, finding a clue in each one that led her to the treasure in the final city. Can you put the list of the eight cities she visited in order, using the information below?

1. The clue in Amsterdam led her immediately to the other city that began with an A.

2. She visited Skopje immediately before visiting Tokyo.

3. She did not find the treasure in Lima, Madrid, or Dodoma.

4. She visited the capital of Peru immediately after visiting the capital of Algeria.

5. Bangkok was one of the first three cities she visited.

6. The capital of Spain was the third city she visited.

7. She visited four other cities between her trips to Dodoma and Skopje.

The Adventure of the Copper Beeches (Part I)

Sherlock Holmes heard the information below from a witness while trying to solve a mystery. Read the text, then turn the page for a quiz on what you've read.

Both Mr. and Mrs. Rucastle...were waiting for me in the drawing room, which is a very large room, stretching along the entire front of the house, with three long windows reaching down to the floor. A chair had been placed close to the central window, with its back turned towards it. In this I was asked to sit, and then Mr. Rucastle, walking up and down on the other side of the room, began to tell me a series of the funniest stories that I have ever listened to. You cannot imagine how comical he was, and I laughed until I was quite weary. Mrs. Rucastle, however, who has evidently no sense of humor, never so much as smiled, but sat with her hands in her lap, and a sad, anxious look upon her face. After an hour or so, Mr. Rucastle suddenly remarked that it was time to commence the duties of the day, and that I might change my dress and go to little Edward in the nursery.

The Adventure of the Copper Beeches (Part II)

(Do not read this until you have read the previous page!)

1. Where were the Rucastles waiting?

    A. The dining room

    B. The front room

    C. The nursery

    D. The drawing room

2. Who told funny stories?

    A. Mr. Rucastle

    B. Mrs. Rucastle

    C. The narrator

    D. Edward

3. How many windows were in the room?

    A. Two

    B. Three

    C. Four

    D. None

4. What was the narrator asked to do in the end, along with going to the nursery?

    A. Feed Edward

    B. Clean the nursery

    C. Change her dress

    D. Call Holmes

130

Answers on page 187.

Missing Piece

Below is a quotation from a Sherlock Holmes story. Rearrange each set of scrambled capital letters to reveal the missing word. Bonus: Name the Sherlock Holmes adventure from which this quotation is drawn.

"Having TREDAGEH _____ these facts, Watson, I SOKEDM _____

several EPPIS _____ over them, trying to TERSAAPE _____

those which were CALICUR _____ from others which were merely

NITEILCDNA _____. There could be no ITQOUNSE _____ that the

most INITVSETCDI _____ and VSESGTIGEU _____ point in the

case was the singular REEDAPASACIPN _____ of the door key.

A most careful CHARES _____ had failed to OVECDIRS _____

it in the room. Therefore it must have been taken from it. But neither the

OCLOLEN _____ nor the Colonel's wife could have taken it.

131

Answers on page 188.

A Wild Night

Below is a quotation from a Sherlock Holmes adventure. Every word or phrase in all capital letters is contained within the group of letters. Words can be found in a straight line horizontally, vertically, or diagonally. They may be read either forward or backward.

I could not SLEEP that night. A vague feeling of IMPENDING misfortune IMPRESSED me. My SISTER and I, you will recollect, were TWINS, and you know how SUBTLE are the links which bind two SOULS which are so closely ALLIED. It was a WILD night. The wind was HOWLING outside, and the rain was BEATING and SPLASHING against the windows. SUDDENLY, amid all the HUBBUB of the gale, there BURST forth the wild SCREAM of a TERRIFIED woman. I knew that it was my sister's voice. I SPRANG from my bed, wrapped a SHAWL round me, and rushed into the CORRIDOR. As I opened my door I seemed to hear a low WHISTLE, such as my sister described, and a few moments later a CLANGING sound, as if a MASS of metal had FALLEN.

– The Adventure of the Speckled Band

```
E N Y J L X O A V R W B H Y W Q P T
P F H S H G X L Y S T U R P E D Y H
A T F J N O R O M Y B O J N Z M V R
N W E A R P W E U B K W S U B T L E
Z A R R L E C L U W H B S S A M U H
Z P F J R Q T B I I M P E N D I N G
S G W N Z I W S S N S A K V S S B W
T N N G S B F T I G G J U P I J K Q
L D N I Q G L I U S S U L I S W Z K
B E P F G E K W E H T A M M N J Z S
E I Z P B N N K A D S R Q P I H I R
A L K W E E A W R H S O I R W S M E
T L L X L E L L I J C D P E T L Q Y
I A O L F P L N C P R I B S I U B G
N M A A W E G S S E E R M S W O P A
G F X I B U R S T P A R G E C S Q S
K F L Y N J M C R U M O P D L F L V
L D Y L N E D D U S Q C A K H I A W
```

133

Answers on page 188.

Fingerprint Match

Find the matching fingerprint(s). There may be more than one.

A.

B.

C.

D.

E.

F.

G.

H.

I.

Dinner with Holmes

Below is a quotation from a Sherlock Holmes story. Rearrange each set of scrambled capital letters to reveal the missing word. Bonus: Name the Sherlock Holmes adventure from which this quotation is drawn.

Our meal was a RYRME _____ one. Holmes could talk

EYGXIDELCNE _____ well when he chose, and that night he did

choose. He appeared to be in a state of nervous LAEITNOAXT _____.

I have never known him so RNBLIITLA _____. He spoke on a quick

succession of subjects—on ERLIAMC _____ plays, on ADELEMIV

_____ pottery, on Stradivarius violins, on the SBUDHMDI _____

of Ceylon, and on the HIRWPSSA _____ of the future—handling

ACHE _____ as though he had made a special study of it. His

GITHBR _____ humor marked the AIRCENOT _____ from his

black depression of the preceding days. Athelney Jones proved to be a

OBESICAL _____ soul in his hours of ERTXLAIANO _____, and

faced his dinner with the air of a bon vivant. For myself, I felt AELTED

_____ at the thought that we were nearing the end of our task, and I

caught something of Holmes's YAGTEI _____.

135

Answers on page 188.

Identity Parade

Mrs. Amnesia was asked to recollect the faces of the 4 suspects who robbed the local bank. Her memory is a bit shaky though. The photos accidentally got put through a shredder, and, currently, only one facial feature in each row is in its correct place. Mrs. Amnesia does know that:

1. B's nose is not next to C's nose.

2. B's hair is one place to the right of B's nose.

3. B's eyes are one place to the right of B's mouth.

4. A's hair is one place to the left of D's mouth.

5. B's eyes are not on the same face as C's nose.

6. C's eyes are one place to the left of C's nose.

Can you find the correct hair, eyes, nose, and mouth for each suspect?

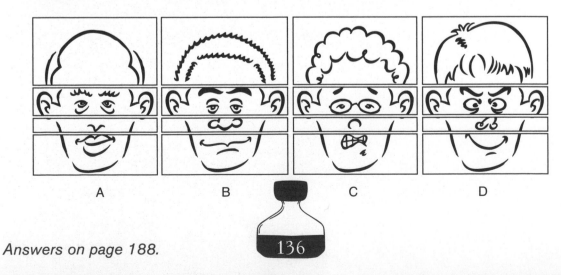

A   B   C   D

Answers on page 188.

Match each Sherlock Holmes short story with the book in which it appears.

1. The Adventures of Sherlock Holmes

2. The Memoirs of Sherlock Holmes

3. The Return of Sherlock Holmes

4. His Last Bow

A. The Adventure of the Devil's Foot

B. The Adventure of the Blue Carbuncle

C. The Adventure of the Second Stain

D. The Adventure of the Resident Patient

Answers on page 188.

Below is a quotation from a Sherlock Holmes adventure. Every word or phrase in all capital letters is contained within the group of letters. Words can be found in a straight line horizontally, vertically, or diagonally. They may be read either forward or backward.

The ROUGH-AND-TUMBLE work in AFGHANISTAN, coming on the top of a natural BOHEMIANISM of disposition, has made me rather more lax than BEFITS a medical man. But with me there is a LIMIT, and when I find a man who keeps his cigars in the COALSCUTTLE, his TOBACCO in the toe end of a Persian SLIPPER, and his UNANSWERED correspondence TRANSFIXED by a JACK-KNIFE into the very center of his wooden MANTELPIECE, then I begin to give myself VIRTUOUS airs. I have always held, too, that PISTOL practice should be distinctly an OPEN-AIR pastime; and when Holmes, in one of his queer HUMORS, would sit in an armchair with his HAIR-TRIGGER and a hundred Boxer CARTRIDGES, and proceed to ADORN the opposite wall with a patriotic V. R. done in BULLET-POCKS, I felt strongly that neither the ATMOSPHERE nor the APPEARANCE of our room was IMPROVED by it.

– The Musgrave Ritual

```
P T E C N A R A E P P A Y X T H E Q
D G N M Q J A C K K N I F E A W H G
Z Q B X A N S L I P P E R F Z W M Y
C D D S Y N T D K P O Y G U K S A S
O E C G R V T H P Z C H K C B B B E
A X L F B O H E M I A N I S M C U G
L I I B F F M V L N O F L Y O A N O
S F M F M L P U I P J L L P G H A C
C S P A B U C S H R I N T J U I N C
U N R D F A T U N M T E X V P I S A
T A O O U A M D I E L U C Y E O W B
T R V R N J H T N L T L O E S P E O
L T E N V P F M U A P B I U D E R T
E S D K K Y T B D Z H I U Q S N E W
A T M O S P H E R E N G S Y A A D D
F R E G G I R T R I A H U T A I E A
Z N L Q N P B E F I T S S O O R W V
B F M H S E G D I R T R A C R L D N
```

139

Answers on page 189.

In the Dark

Cryptograms are messages in substitution code. For example, THE SMART CAT might become FVO QWGDF JGF if F is substituted for **T**, V for **H**, O for **E**, and so on. Bonus: Name the Sherlock Holmes adventure from which this quotation is drawn.

J SFB, DMPJSMOL DFXHE WJGP MF GL PJYD, HFM VYFG MOP

EIYPWMIFH FV KJNPY DMYPPM, KXM VYFG MOP KJWN FV MOP

UPYL OFXDP IH BOIWO BP SJL WFHWPJSPE. J EFFY FQPHPE

JHE DOXM. JH IHDMJHM SJMPY DMPQD WYPQM EFBH MOP

QJDDJCP–DMPQD BOIWO BPYP GPJHM MF KP DISPHM, KXM

BOIWO YPUPYKPYJMPE OJYDOSL MOYFXCO MOP PGQML

OFXDP. OFSGPD WYFXWOPE KJWN JCJIHDM MOP BJSS, JHE I

EIE MOP DJGP, GL OJHE WSFDIHC XQFH MOP OJHESP FV GL

YPUFSUPY. QPPYIHC MOYFXCO MOP CSFFG, I DJB MOP

UJCXP FXMSIHP FV J GJH, J DOJEP KSJWNPY MOJH MOP

KSJWNHPDD FV MOP FQPH EFFY. OP DMFFE VFY JH IHDMJHM,

JHE MOPH OP WYPQM VFYBJYE, WYFXWOIHC, GPHJWIHC,

IHMF MOP YFFG. OP BJD BIMOIH MOYPP LJYED FV XD, MOID

DIHIDMPY VICXYP, JHE I OJE KYJWPE GLDPSV MF GPPM OID

DQYIHC.

Answers on page 189.
140

Read the story below, then turn the page and answer the questions.

Sherlock Holmes overheard the jewelry thief tell his accomplice about the different places where he stashed the loot. He said, "The jade figurine is in a box of old magazines in the basement. The ruby is in the pocket of the bathrobe in the closet. The emeralds are in the dining room hutch inside the water pitcher. The opals are underneath the mattress of the bed in the spare room."

(Do not read this until you have read the previous page!)

Holmes overheard the information about where the stolen loot was stored, but didn't have anywhere to write it down! Answer the questions below to help the investigator remember.

1. How many rubies are there?

   A. 1

   B. 2

   C. 3

   D. More than 1, but we don't know how many.

2. What is found in a box of old magazines?

   A. Jade necklace

   B. Jade figurine

   C. Emeralds

   D. Opals

3. The emeralds are found inside this.

   A. Bathrobe pocket

   B. Water pitcher

   C. Butter dish

   D. Carved box

4. The opals are found here.

   A. Spare room

   B. Dining room

   C. Basement

   D. Closet

Answers on page 189.

Holmes' Dual Nature

Below is a quotation from a Sherlock Holmes story. Rearrange each set of scrambled capital letters to reveal the missing word. Bonus: Name the Sherlock Holmes adventure from which this quotation is drawn.

All the afternoon he sat in the stalls ADWEPPR _____ in the most

perfect SEIPSNAHP _____, gently waving his long, thin fingers in time

to the music, while his gently smiling face and his DLAGINU _____,

dreamy eyes were as unlike those of Holmes the TEHOHDULUSN

_____, Holmes the SLTESERNEL _____, keen-witted, ready-

handed CNMALIIR _____ agent, as it was possible to ICOVEENC

_____. In his RAUNISLG _____ character the dual nature alternately

TEDSSARE _____ itself, and his extreme SASENTCEX _____

and ATNUSSTSEE _____ represented, as I have often thought, the

reaction against the poetic and AEVNMLCTOETPI _____ mood which

occasionally ETREOPIDNDAM _____ in him.

Answers on page 189.

The Adventure of the Beryl Coronet

Choose the correct word or phrase to complete each quote from a Sherlock Holmes adventure.

1. My friend rose _____ from his armchair and stood with his hands in the pockets of his dressing-gown, looking over my shoulder.

   A. Gracefully

   B. Fluidly

   C. Lazily

   D. Excitedly

2. It was a bright, crisp February morning, and the _____ of the day before still lay deep upon the ground.

   A. Snow

   B. Fog

   C. Rain

   D. Ice

3. The gray pavement had been cleaned and scraped, but was still dangerously _____, so that there were fewer passengers than usual.

   A. Uneven

   B. Fog-obscured

   C. Slippery

   D. Damaged

4. Indeed, from the direction of the Metropolitan Station no one was coming save the single gentleman whose _____ conduct had drawn my attention.

   A. Erratic

   B. Sly

   C. Suspicious

   D. Eccentric

Answers on page 189.

Motives for Murder

Unscramble each word or phrase below to reveal a word or phrase that might compel someone to murder.

ACNE EN VEG

EDGER

HI NECTARINE

ALACK LIMB

RAFFIA

HASTY CHOPPY

SAY JOULE

IFFY MAULED

IMITATION DIN

SHELTERING ILK

145

Answers on page 189.

Below is a group of words that, when properly arranged in the blanks, reveal a quote from the Sherlock Holmes story "The Adventure fo the Blue Carbuncle."

ACTION

BIZARRE

COMBINATION

CRIMINAL

PROBLEM

REACTION

SWARM

Amid the _____ and _____ of
so dense a _____ of humanity,
every possible _____ of events
may be expected to take place,
and many a little _____ will be
presented which may be striking and _____ without being
_____.

The Greek Interpreter

Choose the correct word or phrase to complete each quote from a Sherlock Holmes adventure.

1. If the art of the detective began and ended in reasoning from an armchair, my brother would be the greatest _____ agent that ever lived.

   A. Investigative

   B. Political

   C. Secret

   D. Criminal

2. He will not even go out of his way to verify his own _____, and would rather be considered wrong than take the trouble to prove himself right.

   A. Suspicions

   B. Solutions

   C. Informants

   D. Writings

3. Again and again I have taken a problem to him, and have received an explanation which has afterwards proved to be the _____ one.

   A. Correct

   B. Wrong

   C. Silliest

   D. Logical

4. He was absolutely incapable of working out the _____ which must be gone into before a case could be laid before a judge or jury.

   A. Evidence

   B. Inquiries

   C. Practical points

   D. History

147

Answers on page 190.

Motel Hideout

A thief hides out in one of the 45 motel rooms listed in the chart below. Sherlock Holmes received a sheet of four clues, signed "The Holiday Thief." Using these clues, Holmes found the room number within 15 minutes—but by that time, the thief had fled. Can you find the thief's motel room quicker?

1. The first digit and the second digit are one digit apart (e.g, 43, 45).

2. The sum of the digits is 5 or greater.

3. It is divisible by 3.

4. It is less than 7 squared.

51	52	53	54	55	56	57	58	59
41	42	43	44	45	46	47	48	49
31	32	33	34	35	36	37	38	39
21	22	23	24	25	26	27	28	29
11	12	13	14	15	16	17	18	19

Answers on page 190.

Coded Note

Sherlock Holmes just received the letter below, but the writer used a substitution code. For example, THE SMART CAT might become FVO QWGDF JGF if **F** is substituted for **T**, **V** for **H**, **O** for **E**, and so on. Break the code to reveal the message. Bonus: Name the Sherlock Holmes adventure from which this letter is drawn.

VWWSF MJVYMS, HVJQTVH, BSYE

HF PSVJ HJ. TRUHSQ:

Z QTRNUP WS LSJF MUVP RA FRNJ ZHHSPZVES

VQQZQEVYOS ZY KTVE XJRHZQSQ ER WS V HRQE

JSHVJBVWUS OVQS. ZE ZQ QRHSETZYM CNZES

ZY FRNJ UZYS. SIOSXE ARJ JSUSVQZYM ETS UVPF

Z KZUU QSS ETVE SLSJFETZYM ZQ BSXE SIVOEUF

VQ Z TVLS ARNYP ZE, WNE Z WSM FRN YRE ER

URQS VY ZYQEVYE, VQ ZE ZQ PZAAZONUE ER

USVLS QZJ SNQEVOS ETSJS.

FRNJQ AVZETANUUF,

QEVYUSF TRXBZYQ.

Irene Adler

1. What is Irene Adler's trained profession?

    A. Burglar

    B. Opera singer

    C. Lady's companion

    D. Dancer

2. Who hires Holmes to investigate Adler?

    A. Mycroft

    B. The Prince of Sweden

    C. Professor Moriarty

    D. The King of Bohemia

3. What does Holmes request as payment for dealing with Adler?

    A. A recommendation to Scotland Yard

    B. A pardon of Adler's criminal behavior

    C. A picture of Adler

    D. Nothing

4. In how many of Conan Doyle's stories is Adler a character?

    A. One

    B. Two

    C. Three

    D. Five

Answers on page 190.

Read the story below, then turn the page and answer the questions.

A bystander heard two people talking at a coffee shop, only to realize they were counterfeiters! One said to the other, "The order is thirty-five $20 dollar bills, sixty $100 bills, and one hundred $10 bills. I've left it in the safe, and the temporary combination is 03-21-17. You need to pick it up by Thursday at 6 PM or the money is removed."

(Do not read this until you have read the previous page!)

1. How many bills of each denomination are being delivered? (For some, the answer may be zero.)

   $5: _____

   $10: _____

   $20: _____

   $50: _____

   $100: _____

2. What is the combination for the safe?

   _____

3. What is the deadline to pick up the delivery?

   _____

Dr. Watson made the observations below while he and Sherlock Holmes were trying to solve a mystery. Read the text, then turn the page for a quiz on what you've read.

The building was of grey, lichen-blotched stone, with a high central portion and two curving wings, like the claws of a crab, thrown out on each side. In one of these wings the windows were broken and blocked with wooden boards, while the roof was partly caved in, a picture of ruin. The central portion was in little better repair, but the right-hand block was comparatively modern, and the blinds in the windows, with the blue smoke curling up from the chimneys, showed that this was where the family resided. Some scaffolding had been erected against the end wall, and the stonework had been broken into, but there were no signs of any workmen at the moment of our visit. Holmes walked slowly up and down the ill-trimmed lawn and examined with deep attention the outsides of the windows.

The Adventure of the Speckled Band
(Part II)

(Do not read this until you have read the previous page!)

1. To what are the wings of the house compared?

    A. The ruins of a church

    B. The arms of a dancer

    C. The claws of a crab

    D. The blinds of windows

2. How does Watson know where the family resided?

    A. The lights were on

    B. Smoke was coming from the chimneys

    C. He could see them through the windows

    D. There was the noise of socializing

3. In what part of the place did the family life?

    A. The central part

    B. The ground floor

    C. The left wing

    D. The right wing

4. What color is the building's stone?

    A. Black

    B. Grey

    C. White

    D. Brick red

Answers on page 191.

Bank Mayhem

A criminal mastermind who calls himself "Trixter" has hidden a stolen artifact in one of forty-five different safety deposit boxes at the local bank. Each box has a different number, and the miscreant has given the police a series of clues that will point to its hidden location. Using only these clues, find the one correct number – but be careful! Open the wrong box and the priceless artifact will be destroyed.

1. The sum of the digits is greater than 9.

2. The second digit is not prime.

3. It is greater than 60.

4. Both digits multiplied together equals the number immediately below it in the grid.

83	85	87	89	91	93	95	97	99
65	67	69	71	73	75	77	79	81
47	49	51	53	55	57	59	61	63
29	31	33	35	37	39	41	43	45
11	13	15	17	19	21	23	25	27

Answers on page 191.

Below is a quotation from a Sherlock Holmes adventure. Every word or phrase in all capital letters is contained within the group of letters. Words can be found in a straight line horizontally, vertically, or diagonally. They may be read either forward or backward.

During my SCHOOLDAYS I had been intimately ASSOCIATED with a lad named Percy PHELPS, who was of much the same age as myself, though he was two CLASSES ahead of me. He was a very BRILLIANT boy, and carried away every PRIZE which the SCHOOL had to offer, finished his EXPLOITS by winning a SCHOLARSHIP which sent him on to continue his TRIUMPHANT career at CAMBRIDGE. He was, I remember, extremely well CONNECTED, and even when we were all little boys together we knew that his mother's brother was Lord HOLDHURST, the great conservative POLITICIAN. This GAUDY relationship did him little good at school. On the CONTRARY, it seemed rather a PIQUANT thing to us to CHEVY him about the PLAYGROUND and hit him over the shins with a WICKET. But it was another thing when he came out into the WORLD. I heard VAGUELY that his abilities and the INFLUENCES which he commanded had won him a good position at the FOREIGN OFFICE.

– The Naval Treaty

```
I  W  Y  T  S  J  E  G  D  I  R  B  M  A  C  X  J  O
F  S  D  L  B  Q  E  T  I  D  P  Q  G  Q  W  W  F  L
P  O  L  J  Y  R  E  X  E  M  H  W  O  C  P  B  C  V
I  W  R  B  P  K  N  T  P  P  U  D  M  N  U  K  O  T
Q  T  O  E  C  W  A  C  S  L  P  I  J  K  S  C  N  R
U  H  W  I  I  I  V  C  M  I  O  I  J  K  Y  V  T  I
A  T  W  Y  C  G  H  A  H  Z  N  I  C  P  A  H  R  U
N  C  N  O  D  O  N  S  G  F  R  O  T  T  D  Z  A  M
T  P  S  A  O  U  R  O  L  U  N  R  I  S  L  H  R  P
I  S  M  L  I  A  A  U  F  N  E  C  O  R  O  E  Y  H
A  C  B  S  L  L  E  G  E  F  L  L  V  U  O  P  V  A
S  D  H  O  P  N  L  C  Q  M  I  R  Y  H  H  R  S  N
E  R  H  E  C  H  T  I  J  V  H  C  H  D  C  I  P  T
S  C  B  E  V  E  O  E  R  O  B  Y  E  L  S  Z  L  S
S  R  S  Y  D  Y  T  N  S  B  R  Y  Y  O  Q  E  E  S
A  A  N  A  I  C  I  T  I  L  O  P  G  H  Z  N  H  W
L  F  K  H  M  D  I  Y  N  G  W  Y  H  G  I  M  P  X
C  U  Q  P  L  A  Y  G  R  O  U  N  D  D  M  N  K  K
```

157

Answers on page 191.

There are eight sets of fingerprints. Find each match.

A.

B.

C.

D.

E.

F.

G.

H.

I.

J.

K.

L.

M.

N.

O.

P.
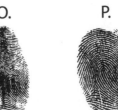

Answers on page 191.

In the End

Below is a quotation from a Sherlock Holmes story. Rearrange each set of scrambled capital letters to reveal the missing word. Bonus: Name the Sherlock Holmes adventure from which this quotation is drawn.

"If my record were closed tonight I could still EVSUYR _____ it with

INTQAYEUMI _____. The air of London is the EETERSW _____

for my CSRNEPEE _____. In over a thousand cases I am not aware

that I have ever used my powers upon the wrong side. Of late I have been

PDMTETE _____ to look into the problems RFHSNUDEI _____ by

nature rather than those more CFRAIPULSIE _____ ones for which

our FLAIAIRCIT _____ state of TOSECYI _____ is responsible.

Your RMIOEMS _____ will draw to an end, Watson, upon the day that I

crown my career by the RUAECTP _____ or TICXOTINNE _____ of

the most dangerous and capable criminal in Europe."

Answers on page 191.

In the Country

Cryptograms are messages in substitution code. Break the code to reveal a quotation from a Sherlock Holmes story. For example, THE SMART CAT might become FVO QWGDF JGF if **F** is substituted for **T**, **V** for **H**, **O** for **E**, and so on. Bonus: Name the Sherlock Holmes adventure from which this quotation is drawn.

"EU FUG NYUJ, JKIRUY," RKAE CV, "ICKI AI AR UYV UB ICV

PGHRVR UB K MAYE JAIC K IGHY ZANV MAYV ICKI A MGRI

ZUUN KI VXVHFICAYQ JAIC HVBVHVYPV IU MF UJY

RSVPAKZ RGWOVPI. FUG ZUUN KI ICVRV RPKIIVHVE

CUGRVR, KYE FUG KHV AMSHVRRVE WF ICVAH WVKGIF. A

ZUUN KI ICVM, KYE ICV UYZF ICUGQCI JCAPC PUMVR IU

MV AR K BVVZAYQ UB ICVAH ARUZKIAUY KYE UB ICV

AMSGYAIF JAIC JCAPC PHAMV MKF WV PUMMAIIVE ICVHV.

. . . ICVF KZJKFR BAZZ MV JAIC K PVHIKAY CUHHUH. AI

AR MF WVZAVB, JKIRUY, BUGYEVE GSUY MF VTSVHAVYPV,

ICKI ICV ZUJVRI KYE XAZVRI KZZVFR AY ZUYEUY EU YUI

SHVRVYI K MUHV EHVKEBGZ HVPUHE UB RAY ICKY EUVR

ICV RMAZAYQ KYE WVKGIABGZ PUGYIHFRAEV."

What Changed? (Part I)

Study this picture for one minute, then turn the page.

What Changed? (Part II)

(Do not read this until you have read the previous page!)

Murder in the kitchen! From memory, can you tell what changed between this and the previous page to pinpoint what was used as a weapon?

Answers on page 191.

Motel Hideout

A thief hides out in one of the 45 motel rooms listed in the chart below. Sherlock Holmes received a sheet of four clues, signed "The Logical Thief." Using these clues, Holmes found the room number within 15 minutes—but by that time, the thief had fled. Can you find the thief's motel room quicker?

1. It is not divisible by 5.

2. It is divisible by 3.

3. The first digit is larger than the second.

4. The second digit is greater than 2.

51	52	53	54	55	56	57	58	59
41	42	43	44	45	46	47	48	49
31	32	33	34	35	36	37	38	39
21	22	23	24	25	26	27	28	29
11	12	13	14	15	16	17	18	19

Answers on page 192.

Below is a quotation from a Sherlock Holmes adventure. Every word or phrase in all capital letters is contained within the group of letters. Words can be found in a straight line horizontally, vertically, or diagonally. They may be read either forward or backward.

In glancing over the somewhat INCOHERENT series of MEMOIRS with which I have endeavored to ILLUSTRATE a few of the mental PECULIARITIES of my FRIEND Mr. Sherlock Holmes, I have been struck by the DIFFICULTY which I have experienced in picking out EXAMPLES which shall in every way answer my purpose. For in those cases in which HOLMES has PERFORMED some TOUR-DE-FORCE of ANALYTICAL reasoning, and has demonstrated the value of his peculiar methods of INVESTIGATION, the FACTS themselves have often been so SLIGHT or so COMMONPLACE that I could not feel JUSTIFIED in laying them before the PUBLIC. On the other hand, it has frequently happened that he has been CONCERNED in some RESEARCH where the facts have been of the most REMARKABLE and DRAMATIC character, but where the share which he has himself taken in determining their CAUSES has been less PRONOUNCED than I, as his BIOGRAPHER, could wish.

– The Resident Patient

```
A V S P F I F U L A C I T Y L A N A
F B D D S X L P U L Y P O I P D P F
S E E R R L K L O S E S S T E G U A
N L C A P W I O U R E E N U F B C
Y B N M R R G G F S I L R S Y G L T
T A U A F G R O H T T E P I U E I S
L K O T T I R E I T C R N M T A C O
U R N I X M U R H N L N A W A F C D
C A O C E V A M O P F G D T R X J F
I M R D B I Z C L Q A J O I E O E N
F E P J L I N C O H E R E N T P N L
F R P U C S E M L O H N G J I O L M
I D C U T S O D X C D R B O E R M E
D E S T O U R D E F O R C E I P O M
P Q J U S T I F I E D B O K R B M O
K I N V E S T I G A T I O N S I J I
G E X R B A Y O R E S E A R C H G R
T S B U B F E C A L P N O M M O C S
```

165

Answers on page 192.

Sherlock

ACROSS

1. Canvas cover?
6. "The March King" John Philip ___
11. Comforter
12. Arm bones
13. Benedict ___ is Holmes in "Sherlock"
15. Remarked
16. Angry feeling
17. Mrs. Hudson is played by ___ Stubbs
20. Lincoln's debate opponent
22. Gallup, Harris or Roper
24. Comic strip lightbulb
25. The E of HOMES
29. Assign to an obscure place
33. Act of deliberate betrayal
36. Big initials in fashion
37. "Awesome!" in the '80s
38. Kennedy and Danson
40. He plays criminal mastermind Jim Moriarty in "Sherlock"
45. "Murder, She Wrote" setting
46. Where Ephesus was located
47. Boiling pot's output
48. Short online posting

DOWN

1. Chest muscle, for short
2. Sports org. for nonprofessionals
3. Political doctrine
4. Birds' beaks
5. Sneaker patterns
6. Bring under control
7. Commercial ending for Cray- or Motor
8. No later than
9. Pelvic bones
10. Volcanic residue
14. One who really makes you laugh
17. AP rival, once
18. Agree wordlessly
19. Pint in a pub
21. Rupert Graves plays DI ___ Lestrade
23. Irene Adler, "The Woman," is played by ___ Pulver in "Sherlock"
26. "The Martian Chronicles" author Bradbury
27. Manilow's "___ a Miracle"
28. Slippery swimmer
30. Hold in regard
31. M-G-M co-founder Marcus
32. Breaks up a relationship
33. Aerial railway cars
34. Charged, as a bull
35. Funny Murphy
39. Trash-hauling boat
41. Cell "messenger," briefly
42. Number that's its own square root
43. All-even score
44. Work at lace-making

Answers on page 192.

Police Station Shenanigans

A criminal known as the Trixster has hidden a stolen brooch in a vending machine right in the waiting room of the precinct! Each option in the vending machine has its own number, and "Trixter" has given the police a series of clues that will reveal its exact location. Can you retrieve the stolen brooch?

1. It is not a multiple of 5.

2. It is greater than 30.

3. It is a multiple of 7.

4. The sum of the digits is less than 10.

11	12	13	14	15	16	17	18	19
21	22	23	24	25	26	27	28	29
31	32	33	34	35	36	37	38	39
41	42	43	44	45	46	47	48	49
51	52	53	54	55	56	57	58	59

Answers on page 192.

Choose the correct word or phrase to complete each quote from a Sherlock Holmes adventure.

1. A man entered who could hardly have been less than six feet six inches in height, with the chest and limbs of a _____.

   A. Perseus

   B. Hercules

   C. Atlas

   D. Achilles

2. His dress was rich with a _____ which would, in England, be looked upon as akin to bad taste.

   A. Sparkle

   B. Plushness

   C. Brightness

   D. Richness

3. The deep blue cloak which was thrown over his shoulders was lined with _____-colored silk and secured at the neck with a brooch which consisted of a single flaming beryl.

   A. Flame

   B. Brick

   C. Silver

   D. Gold

4. He carried a _____ in his hand, while he wore across the upper part of his face, extending down past the cheekbones, a black vizard mask.

   A. Curved dagger

   B. Monogrammed handkerchief

   C. Broad-brimmed hat

   D. Thickly furred overcoat

Answers on page 192.

The Showdown

Cryptograms are messages in substitution code. For example, THE SMART CAT might become FVO QWGDF JGF if **F** is substituted for **T**, **V** for **H**, **O** for **E**, and so on. Bonus: Name the Sherlock Holmes adventure from which this quotation is drawn.

AZC, WU W MZKHX PDNQ XZAQ SPWL CWSPZKS SPQ RAZCH-QXVQ ZU EYZUQLLZY GZYWDYSJ, DHH CZKHX PDNQ IQQA CQHH. IKS PQ CDL SZZ CWHJ UZY SPDS. PQ LDC QNQYJ LSQE CPWMP W SZZR SZ XYDC GJ SZWHL YZKAX PWG. DVDWA DAX DVDWA PQ LSYZNQ SZ IYQDR DCDJ, IKS W DL ZUSQA PQDXQX PWG ZUU. W SQHH JZK, GJ UYWQAX, SPDS WU D XQSDWHQX DMMZKAS ZU SPDS LWHQAS MZASQLS MZKHX IQ CYWSSQA, WS CZKHX SDRQ WSL EHDMQ DL SPQ GZLS IYWHHWDAS IWS ZU SPYKLS-DAX-EDYYJ CZYR WA SPQ PWLSZYJ ZU XQSQMSWZA. AQNQY PDNQ W YWLQA SZ LKMP D PQWVPS, DAX AQNQY PDNQ W IQQA LZ PDYX EYQLLQX IJ DA ZEEZAQAS. PQ MKS XQQE, DAX JQS W OKLS KAX-QYMKS PWG. SPWL GZYAWAV SPQ HDLS LSQEL CQYQ SDRQA, DAX SPYQQ XDJL ZAHJ CQYQ CDASQX SZ MZGEHQSQ SPQ IKL-WAQLL. W CDL LWSSWAV WA GJ YZZG SPWARWAV SPQ GDSSQY ZNQY, CPQA SPQ XZZY ZEQAQX DAX EYZUQLLZY GZYWDYSJ LSZZX IQUZYQ GQ.

Answer Key

Hidden Spot (page 4)

"Now, Watson, now!" cried Holmes with FRENZIED eagerness. All the DEMONIACAL force of the man MASKED behind that LISTLESS manner burst out in a PAROXYSM of energy. He tore the drugget from the FLOOR, and in an instant was down on his hands and knees CLAWING at each of the SQUARES of wood beneath it. One turned SIDEWAYS as he dug his nails into the edge of it. It HINGED back like the lid of a box. A small black CAVITY opened beneath it. Holmes plunged his EAGER hand into it and drew it out with a bitter SNARL of ANGER and DISAPPOINTMENT. It was EMPTY.

Story: The Adventure of the Second Stain

Where the Evidence Leads Us (page 5)

Circumstantial evidence is a very tricky thing. It may seem to point very straight to one thing, but if you shift your own point of view a little, you may find it pointing in an equally uncompromising manner to something entirely different. – Arthur Conan Doyle, The Adventures of Sherlock Holmes

Interception (page 6)

Take the second letter of each word to reveal: Barcelona

Say What? (page 7)

It was not that he felt any emotion akin to love for Irene Adler. All emotions, and that one particularly, were abhorrent to his cold, precise, but admirably balanced mind.

Say What? (page 7)

Life is infinitely stranger than anything which the mind of man could invent. We would not dare to conceive the things which are really mere commonplaces of existence.

Mysterious Motive (page 8)

"What is the meaning of it, Watson?" said Holmes solemnly as he laid down the paper. "What object is served by this circle of misery and violence and fear? It must tend to some end, or else our universe is ruled by chance, which is unthinkable. But what end? There is the great standing perennial problem to which human reason is as far from an answer as ever."

– The Adventure of the Cardboard Box

Answer Key

Overheard Information (Part II) (page 10)

1. A; 2. D; 3. C; 4. A

Baker Street Revisited (page 14)

S	L	A	B	■	■	■	T	H	E	M	E
H	E	L	L	S	■	B	R	A	V	E	D
A	V	I	A	N	■	A	I	L	I	N	G
W	I	T	H	O	U	T	A	C	L	U	E
■	■	■	S	O	R	E	L	Y	■	■	■
A	F	T	■	Z	E	D	■	O	V	E	R
I	R	E	N	E	■	■	A	N	I	T	A
M	Y	N	A	■	A	N	G	■	A	C	E
■	■	■	M	O	R	A	L	S	■	■	■
E	N	T	E	R	T	H	E	L	I	O	N
A	O	R	T	A	S	■	A	I	S	L	E
T	R	E	A	T	Y	■	M	E	L	D	S
S	I	E	G	E	■	■	■	R	E	S	T

The Murderous Gem Thief (page 11)

The count is: 1 diamond, 2 rubies, 3 amethysts, 4 garnets, and 5 peridots.

Dramatic Entrance (page 12)

Y	D	Q	P	A	N	Q	D	D	I	G	N	I	F	I	E	D	I	E	E
N	E	F	W	O	T	E	I	F	L	O	H	L	R	Q	L	A	N	M	L
Y	J	T	I	S	M	H	G	Y	I	Y	T	X	S	N	U	K	R	B	B
J	P	T	A	E	O	L	O	T	P	E	D	E	D	Q	F	W	B	O	I
W	C	O	E	R	E	L	S	R	E	H	C	H	E	X	B	N	E	D	S
A	V	S	M	O	T	E	I	R	N	O	Q	Y	X	H	B	N	A	I	N
S	U	W	K	P	J	S	T	D	N	E	I	O	I	Z	Z	N	R	M	E
U	T	T	G	A	O	S	O	D	I	Z	Y	T	T	Y	G	E	S	E	S
T	F	A	M	P	R	U	S	R	N	T	U	C	S	C	U	R	K	N	N
C	U	U	G	E	L	P	S	O	P	F	Y	Q	R	L	V	O	I	T	U
E	W	F	K	E	F	D	R	A	M	A	T	I	C	O	K	O	N	U	O
L	X	A	A	T	H	S	L	I	P	P	E	D	A	I	F	D	X	C	W
L	B	P	A	P	P	E	A	R	A	N	C	E	U	F	D	T	K	O	P
O	T	S	E	T	N	P	R	S	N	O	I	T	C	N	I	T	S	I	D
C	O	Q	X	O	H	N	K	E	N	T	Q	M	G	P	S	G	Q	H	L
E	I	Y	L	R	W	G	S	Y	G	E	D	S	Z	O	K	B	R	I	C
B	H	P	W	U	L	J	I	N	S	G	D	R	A	X	J	D	X	Y	E
T	R	U	J	F	N	C	C	E	O	Z	A	D	E	S	T	G	J	L	D
I	Y	C	E	V	A	A	E	Z	W	J	A	T	U	E	Y	N	M	P	J
K	C	G	N	I	L	T	R	A	T	S	W	H	S	S	U	Q	M	W	Q

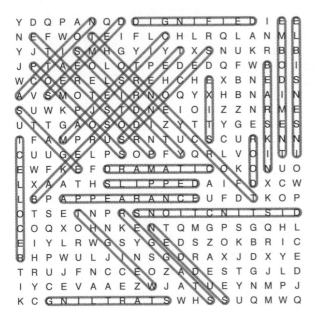

Interception (page 16)

Take the central letter of each place name and the result is BERLIN.

What Changed? (Part II) (page 18)

An extra knife was snuck into the collection!

Answer Key

The Adventure of the Blue Carbuncle
(Part II) (page 20)

1. A; 2. C; 3. B; 4. C

Domestic Logic (page 21)

Mr. Linus lives in House E.

Mycroft Holmes (page 22)

1. B; 2. C; 3. B; 4. A

Shades of Red (page 23)

From north, south, east, and west every man who had a SHADE of red in his hair had TRAMPED into the city to ANSWER the ADVERTISEMENT. Fleet Street was CHOKED with red-headed folk, and Pope's COURT looked like a coster's orange BARROW. I should not have thought there were so many in the whole COUNTRY as were brought TOGETHER by that single ADVERTISEMENT. Every shade of color they were—straw, LEMON, orange, BRICK, Irish-setter, LIVER, clay.

Story: The Red-Headed League

Pick Your Poison (page 24)

From left to right, the bottles are: largest, medium, medium, medium, smallest. The poison is found in the middle, medium-size bottle.

Facing Facts (page 25)

"My dear Watson," said he, "I cannot agree with those who rank modesty among the virtues. To the logician all things should be seen exactly as they are, and to underestimate one's self is as much a departure from truth as to exaggerate one's own powers. When I say, therefore, that Mycroft has better powers of observation than I, you may take it that I am speaking the exact and literal truth."

– The Greek Interpreter

Answer Key

Criminals (page 26)

bandit

burglar

crook

gangster

mugger

outlaw

robber

thief

Fingerprint Match (page 27)

E, L, and N are the matching fingerprints.

Collection of Cases (page 28)

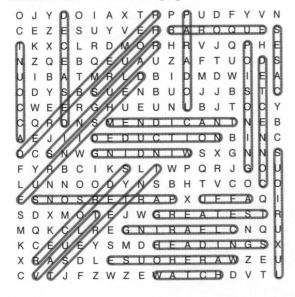

Moriarty Appears (page 30)

"He is EXTREMELY tall and thin, his FOREHEAD domes out in a white CURVE, and his two eyes are deeply sunken in his head. He is clean-shaven, pale, and ASCETIC-looking, retaining SOMETHING of the PROFESSOR in his features. His SHOULDERS are ROUNDED from much study, and his face PROTRUDES forward, and is forever slowly OSCILLATING from side to side in a curiously REPTILIAN fashion. He peered at me with great CURIOSITY in his PUCKERED eyes."

Story: The Final Problem

Overheard Information (Part II) (page 32)

1. B. The 21st; 2. D. A location is not given. 3. B. False; 4. C. Diner

The Adventure of the Noble Bachelor (Part II) (page 34)

1. C; 2. B; 3. A; 4. A

Answer Key

The Murderous Gem Thief (page 35)

The count is: 1 turquoise, 2 diamonds, 3 sapphires, 4 rubies, and 5 pieces of topaz.

Catch the Thief (page 38)

The missing letter is A.

Departure, Paris, Wednesday, airplane

The Cost of Secrets (page 36)

"Well, my dear sir, KNOWING the VINDICTIVE character of his old ASSOCIATES, he was trying to hide his own IDENTITY from EVERYBODY as long as he could. His secret was a SHAMEFUL one, and he could not bring himself to DIVULGE it. However, WRETCH as he was, he was still living under the shield of BRITISH law, and I have no doubt, INSPECTOR, that you will see that, though that SHIELD may fail to guard, the SWORD of JUSTICE is still there to avenge."

–   The RESIDENT Patient

The Adventure of the Dancing Men (Part II) (page 40)

1. D; 2. C; 3. A; 4. D

Stop and Smell the Roses (page 37)

He walked past the couch to the open window, and held up the drooping stalk of a moss-rose, looking down at the dainty blend of crimson and green. It was a new phase of his character to me, for I had never before seen him show any keen interest in natural objects.

–   The Naval Treaty

Train Station Terrors (page 41)

The answer is 27.

Answer Key

On the Scent (page 42)

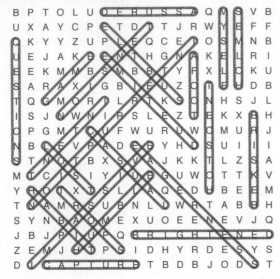

Say What? (page 44)

If we could fly out of that window hand in hand, hover over this great city, gently remove the roofs, and peep in at the queer things which are going on, the strange coincidences, the plannings, the cross-purposes, the wonderful chains of events, working through generations, and leading to the most outré results, it would make all fiction with its conventionalities and foreseen conclusions most stale and unprofitable.

Fingerprint Match (page 45)

C, F, and I are matches.

Holmes on His Own (page 46)

I had seen little of Holmes lately. My MARRIAGE had drifted us away from each other. My own complete HAPPINESS, and the home-centered INTERESTS which rise up around the man who first finds himself master of his own ESTABLISHMENT, were sufficient to absorb all my attention, while Holmes, who LOATHED every form of society with his whole BOHEMIAN soul, remained in our lodgings in Baker Street, buried among his old books, and alternating from week to week between cocaine and AMBITION, the DROWSINESS of the drug, and the fierce energy of his own keen nature. He was still, as ever, deeply ATTRACTED by the study of crime, and occupied his immense FACULTIES and EXTRAORDINARY powers of observation in following out those clues, and clearing up those MYSTERIES which had been ABANDONED as HOPELESS by the official police.

Story: Scandal in Bohemia

Sherlock's Retirement (page 47)

1. A; 2. B; 3. D; 4. C

Coded Letter (page 48)

If you will only come round at quarter to twelve

to the east gate you will learn what

will very much surprise you and maybe

be of the greatest service to you and also

to Annie Morrison. But say nothing to anyone

upon the matter

Story: The Reigate Squires

Answer Key

Treasure Hunt (page 49)

The order is: Singapore, Paris, New York City, London, Bogota, and Nairobi.

The Reigate Squires (page 53)

1. B; 2. A; 3. D; 4. C

Which Adventure? (page 50)

1. D; 2. B; 3. C; 4. A

Crack the Code (page 54)

The missing letter is V.

Solve, evidence, investigate, detective, thieves

The Adventure of the Priory School (Part II) (page 52)

1. C; 2. A; 3. D; 4. B

Crime Cryptogram (page 54)

The actor's costar accused him of a dastardly crime, but the police refused to investigate. What did he do?

He stole the scene!

Answer Key

Mysterious Force (page 55)

"As you are aware, Watson, there is no one who knows the HIGHER criminal world of LONDON so well as I do. For years past I have CONTINUALLY been CONSCIOUS of some power behind the MALEFACTOR, some deep ORGANIZING power which FOREVER stands in the way of the law and throws its SHIELD over the wrong doer. Again and again in cases of the most varying sorts—FORGERY cases, ROBBERIES, MURDERS—I have felt the presence of this force, and I have deduced its action in many of those UNDISCOVERED crimes in which I have not been personally CONSULTED. For years I have ENDEAVORED to break through the veil which shrouded it, and at last the time came when I seized my THREAD and followed it, until it led me, after a thousand cunning WINDINGS, to ex-Professor Moriarty of MATHEMATICAL celebrity.

Story: The Final Problem

Say What? (page 56)

I had no keener pleasure than in following Holmes in his professional investigations, and in admiring the rapid deductions, as swift as intuitions, and yet always founded on a logical basis, with which he unraveled the problems which were submitted to him.

Pick Your Poison (page 57)

From left to right, the bottles are orange, blue, yellow, green, and red. The poison is found in the blue bottle.

Motel Hideout (page 58)

The thief is in room 59.

Interception (page 59)

Take the first letter of the first word, the last letter of the second word, the first letter of the third word, and the last letter of the fourth word. Continue, alternating between the first letter of one word and the final letter of the next word, until you have the whole message: Cottage Grove Inn, Room Eight

When Holmes Is Bored (page 60)

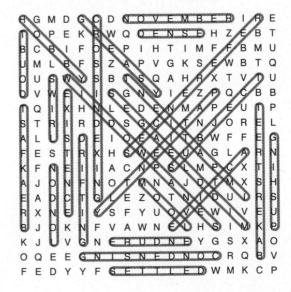

178

Answer Key

Most Unusual (page 62)

"As a rule," said Holmes, "the more bizarre a thing is the less mysterious it proves to be. It is your commonplace, featureless crimes which are really puzzling, just as a commonplace face is the most difficult to identify.

Story: The Read-Headed League

Treasure Hunt (page 63)

The order is: amethysts, gold bars, silver coins, rubies, diamonds, sapphires.

Holmes Books (page 64)

1. B; 2. C; 3. D; 4. A

What Changed? (Part II) (page 66)

The cap on the bottle on the left disappeared.

Once the Solution Is Found (page 67)

I have mentioned somewhere in these incoherent memoirs, the outbursts of passionate energy when he performed the remarkable feats with which his name is associated were followed by reactions of lethargy during which he would lie about with his violin and his books, hardly moving save from the sofa to the table.

– The Musgrave Ritual

Interception (page 68)

Take the central letter of each word and you get NILBUD. Flip this, and it becomes DUBLIN.

Answer Key

Stormy Night (page 69)

It was a wild, TEMPESTUOUS night, towards the close of NOVEMBER. Holmes and I sat together in SILENCE all the evening, he engaged with a powerful lens DECIPHERING the remains of the original INSCRIPTION upon a PALIMPSEST, I deep in a recent TREATISE upon SURGERY. Outside the wind howled down Baker Street, while the rain beat fiercely against the windows. It was STRANGE there, in the very depths of the town, with ten miles of man's HANDIWORK on every side of us, to feel the iron grip of NATURE, and to be conscious that to the huge ELEMENTAL forces all London was no more than the MOLEHILLS that dot the fields.

Story: The Adventure of the Golden Pince-Nez

A Convincing Facade (page 73)

As I entered, I saw, it is true, an unwonted tidiness, but the old landmarks were all in their place. There were the chemical corner and the acid-stained, deal-topped table. There upon a shelf was the row of formidable scrapbooks and books of reference which many of our fellow citizens would have been so glad to burn. The diagrams, the violin-case, and the pipe-rack—even the Persian slipper which contained the tobacco—all met my eyes as I glanced round me. There were two occupants of the room—one, Mrs. Hudson, who beamed upon us both as we entered—the other, the strange dummy which had played so important a part in the evening's adventures. It was a wax-colored model of my friend, so admirably done that it was a perfect facsimile. It stood on a small pedestal table with an old dressing-gown of Holmes's so draped round it that the illusion from the street was absolutely perfect.

Story: The Adventure of the Empty House

Professor Moriarty (page 70)

1. C; 2. D; 3. B; 4. B

In the Collection (page 74)

1. D; 2. A; 3. B; 4. C

Overheard Information (Part II) (page 72)

1. True; 2. False; 3. False; 4. True

Domestic Logic (page 75)

Mr. Jones lives in House D.

Answer Key

Across the Moors (page 76)

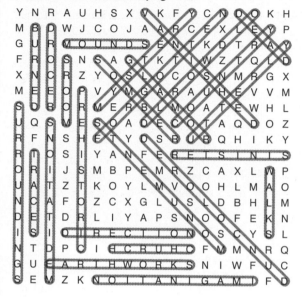

Annoying Mystery (page 81)

All that day and the next and the next Holmes was in a mood which his friends would call TACITURN, and others MOROSE. He ran out and ran in, smoked INCESSANTLY, played snatches on his violin, sank into REVERIES, devoured SANDWICHES at irregular hours, and hardly answered the CASUAL questions which I put to him. It was evident to me that things were not going well with him or his quest. He would say nothing of the case, and it was from the PAPERS that I learned the PARTICULARS of the INQUEST, and the arrest with the SUBSEQUENT release of John Mitton, the valet of the DECEASED. The coroner's jury brought in the OBVIOUS Willful Murder, but the PARTIES remained as unknown as ever.

Story: The Adventure of the Second Stain

Say What? (page 78)

I...was deep in one of Clark Russell's fine sea-stories, until the howl of the gale from without seemed to blend with the text, and the splash of the rain to lengthen out into the long swash of the sea waves.

Crime...and Logic (page 82)

Crime is common. Logic is rare. Therefore it is upon the logic rather than upon the crime that you should dwell. – Sir Arthur Conan Doyle, The Adventure of the Copper Beeches

Overheard Information (Part II) (page 80)

1. A; 2. C; 3. B; 4. D

Where It Happened (page 83)

1. A; 2. C; 3. D; 4. B

Answer Key

Coded Note (page 84)

The missing letter is I.

Diamonds, tiara, diadem, figurine

The Adventure of the Second Stain
(Part II) (page 86)

1. B; 2. A; 3. B; 4. D

Everyone's a Critic (page 87)

I must admit, Watson, that you have some power of SELECTION, which ATONES for much which I DEPLORE in your NARRATIVES. Your FATAL habit of looking at everything from the point of view of a story instead of as a SCIENTIFIC exercise has ruined what might have been an INSTRUCTIVE and even CLASSICAL series of DEMONSTRATIONS. You SLUR over work of the utmost FINESSE and DELICACY, in order to dwell upon SENSATIONAL details which may excite, but cannot possibly instruct, the reader.

Story: The Adventure of the Abbey Grange

Holmes and Watson (page 88)

1. A; 2. C; 3. D; 4. A

Fingerprint Match (page 89)

E is the matching fingerprint.

Mrs. Hudson (page 90)

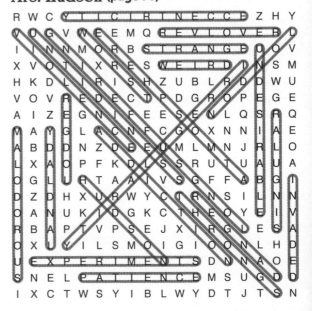

Answer Key

Motel Hideout (page 92)

The thief is in room 24.

The Adventure of the Empty House
(Part II) (page 94)

1. A; 2. B; 3. D; 4. D

Who Is Moriarty? (page 95)

He is the Napoleon of crime, Watson. He is the organizer of half that is evil and of nearly all that is undetected in this great city. He is a genius, a philosopher, an abstract thinker. He has a brain of the first order. He sits motionless, like a spider in the center of its web, but that web has a thousand radiations, and he knows well every quiver of each of them.

– The Final Problem

Find the Witness (page 96)

Chin lives in house D.

Country Vicar (page 97)

I have said that SCATTERED towers marked the VILLAGES which DOTTED this part of Cornwall. The NEAREST of these was the HAMLET of Tredannick Wollas, where the cottages of a couple of hundred inhabitants clustered round an ANCIENT, moss-grown church. The vicar of the parish, Mr. Roundhay, was something of an ARCHEOLOGIST, and as such Holmes had made his ACQUAINTANCE. He was a middle-aged man, PORTLY and AFFABLE, with a CONSIDERABLE fund of local lore. At his invitation we had taken tea at the VICARAGE and had come to know, also, Mr. Mortimer Tregennis, an INDEPENDENT gentleman, who INCREASED the clergyman's scanty RESOURCES by taking rooms in his large, STRAGGLING house.

Story: The Adventure of the Devil's Foot

Locked Door (page 98)

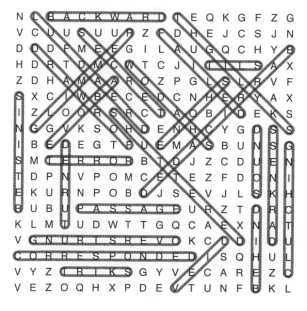

183

Answer Key

They Played Sherlock (page 100)

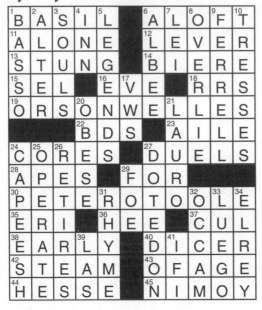

Patience (page 104)

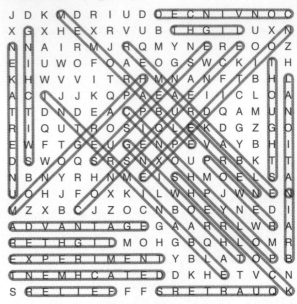

Say What? (page 102)

"The ideal reasoner," [Holmes] remarked, "would, when he had once been shown a single fact in all its bearings, deduce from it not only all the chain of events which led up to it, but also all the results which would follow from it."

Interception (page 106)

In each word, find the letter that occurs twice, and you end up with: Library, Monday

The Murderous Gem Thief (page 103)

The count is: 1 diamond, 2 pearls, 3 rubies, 4 sapphires, and 5 pieces of jade.

The Resident Patient (Part II) (page 108)

1. C; 2. B; 3. A; 4. B

Answer Key

Pick Your Poison (page 109)

From left to right, the bottles are purple, yellow, red, and green. The poison is found in the purple bottle.

All Set (page 110)

Sherlock Holmes was, as I expected, lounging about his sitting-room in his dressing-gown, reading the agony column of The Times and smoking his before-breakfast pipe, which was composed of all the plugs and dottles left from his smokes of the day before, all carefully dried and collected on the corner of the mantelpiece. He received us in his quietly genial fashion, ordered fresh rashers and eggs, and joined us in a hearty meal. When it was concluded he settled our new acquaintance upon the sofa, placed a pillow beneath his head, and laid a glass of brandy and water within his reach.

Story: The Adventure of the Engineer's Thumb

Holmes Pop Quiz (page 111)

1. C; 2. D; 3. A; 4. B

Conan Doyle and Characters (page 112)

1. B; 2. A; 3. D; 4. C

Overheard Information (Part II) (page 114)

1. B; 2. D; 3. A; D. 4. C

On the Scene (page 115)

It was my first visit to the SCENE of the CRIME—a high, DINGY, narrow-chested HOUSE, prim, FORMAL, and solid, like the CENTURY which gave it birth. Lestrade's BULLDOG features gazed out at us from the front window, and he greeted us WARMLY when a big CONSTABLE had opened the door and let us in. The room into which we were shown was that in which the crime had been committed, but no trace of it now remained save an ugly, IRREGULAR stain upon the carpet. This carpet was a small SQUARE drugget in the center of the room, surrounded by a BROAD expanse of BEAUTIFUL, old-fashioned wood flooring in square blocks, highly polished. Over the FIREPLACE was a MAGNIFICENT trophy of WEAPONS, one of which had been used on that tragic night. In the window was a SUMPTUOUS writing desk, and every detail of the APARTMENT, the PICTURES, the rugs, and the HANGINGS, all pointed to a taste which was LUXURIOUS.

Story: The Adventure of the Second Stain

Answer Key

Identity Parade (page 116)

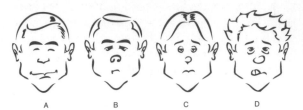

A   B   C   D

Say What? (page 120)

"To the man who loves art for its own sake," remarked Sherlock Holmes, tossing aside the advertisement sheet of The Daily Telegraph, "it is frequently in its least important and lowliest manifestations that the keenest pleasure is to be derived."

Bank Mayhem (page 117)

The answer is 51.

The Adventure of Charles Augustus Milverton (page 121)

1. B; 2. A; 3. D; 4. C

Blue Carbuncle (page 118)

Domestic Logic (page 122)

Mr. Foreman lives in House A.

Answer Key

A Hidden Cache (page 123)

It was a small tin CASHBOX which stood upon the writing desk. Holmes PRIED it open with his CHISEL. Several rolls of paper were within, covered with FIGURES and CALCULATIONS, without any note to show to what they referred. The RECURRING words, "water PRESSURE" and "PRESSURE to the square inch" suggested some possible RELATION to a SUBMARINE. Holmes TOSSED them all IMPATIENTLY aside. There only remained an ENVELOPE with some small NEWSPAPER slips inside it.

Story: The Adventure of the Bruce-Partington Plans

Cleaning Up (page 127)

One winter's night, as we sat together by the fire, I ventured to suggest to him that, as he had finished pasting extracts into his common-place book, he might employ the next two hours in making our room a little more habitable. He could not deny the justice of my request, so with a rather rueful face he went off to his bedroom, from which he returned presently pulling a large tin box behind him. This he placed in the middle of the floor and, squatting down upon a stool in front of it, he threw back the lid. I could see that it was already a third full of bundles of paper tied up with red tape into separate packages.

Story: The Musgrave Ritual

The Murderous Gem Thief (page 124)

The count is: 1 aquamarine, 2 pieces of jade, 3 sapphires, 4 topazes, 5 diamonds, 6 rubies, and 7 emeralds.

Treasure Hunt (page 128)

The order is: Bangkok (Thailand); Dodoma (Tanzania); Madrid (Spain); Amsterdam (Netherlands); Algiers (Algeria); Lima (Peru); Skopje (Macedonia), and Tokyo (Japan).

What Changed? (Part II) (page 126)

A curved knife in the bottom row changed direction.

The Adventure of the Copper Beeches (Part II) (page 130)

1. d; 2. a; 3. b; 4. c

Answer Key

Missing Piece (page 131)

"Having GATHERED these facts, Watson, I SMOKED several PIPES over them, trying to SEPARATE those which were CRUCIAL from others which were merely INCIDENTAL. There could be no QUESTION that the most DISTINCTIVE and SUGGESTIVE point in the case was the singular DISAPPEARANCE of the door key. A most careful SEARCH had failed to DISCOVER it in the room. Therefore it must have been taken from it. But neither the COLONEL nor the Colonel's wife could have taken it.

Story: The Crooked Man

A Wild Night (page 132)

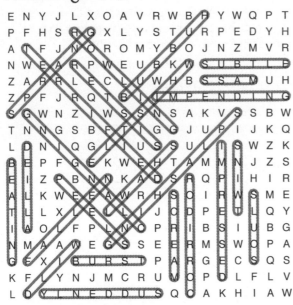

Fingerprint Match (page 134)

F is the matching fingerprint.

Dinner with Holmes (page 135)

Our meal was a MERRY one. Holmes could talk EXCEEDINGLY well when he chose, and that night he did choose. He appeared to be in a state of nervous EXALTATION. I have never known him so BRILLIANT. He spoke on a quick succession of subjects—on MIRACLE plays, on MEDIEVAL pottery, on Stradivarius violins, on the BUDDHISM of Ceylon, and on the WARSHIPS of the future—handling EACH as though he had made a special study of it. His BRIGHT humor marked the REACTION from his black depression of the preceding days. Athelney Jones proved to be a SOCIABLE soul in his hours of RELAXATION, and faced his dinner with the air of a bon vivant. For myself, I felt ELATED at the thought that we were nearing the end of our task, and I caught something of Holmes's GAIETY.

Story: The Sign of Four

Identity Parade (page 136)

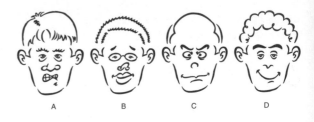

A   B   C   D

In the Collection II (page 137)

1. B; 2. D; 3. C; 4. A

Answer Key

Holmes' Habits (page 138)

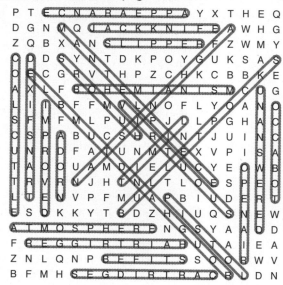

In the Dark (page 140)

A low, stealthy sound came to my ears, not from the direction of Baker Street, but from the back of the very house in which we lay concealed. A door opened and shut. An instant later steps crept down the passage—steps which were meant to be silent, but which reverberated harshly through the empty house. Holmes crouched back against the wall, and I did the same, my hand closing upon the handle of my revolver. Peering through the gloom, I saw the vague outline of a man, a shade blacker than the blackness of the open door. He stood for an instant, and then he crept forward, crouching, menacing, into the room. He was within three yards of us, this sinister figure, and I had braced myself to meet his spring.

Story: The Adventure of the Empty House

Overheard Information (Part II) (page 142)

1. A; 2. B; 3. B; 4. A

Holmes' Dual Nature (page 143)

All the afternoon he sat in the stalls WRAPPED in the most perfect HAPPINESS, gently waving his long, thin fingers in time to the music, while his gently smiling face and his LANGUID, dreamy eyes were as unlike those of Holmes the SLEUTHHOUND, Holmes the RELENTLESS, keen-witted, ready-handed CRIMINAL agent, as it was possible to CONCEIVE. In his SINGULAR character the dual nature alternately ASSERTED itself, and his extreme EXACTNESS and ASTUTENESS represented, as I have often thought, the reaction against the poetic and CONTEMPLATIVE mood which occasionally PREDOMINATED in him.

Story: The Red-Headed League

The Adventure of the Beryl Coronet (page 144)

1. C; 2. A; 3. C; 4. D

Motives for Murder (page 145)

Vengeance; greed; inheritance; blackmail; affair; psychopathy; jealousy; family feud; intimidation; thrill seeking

Answer Key

Say What? (page 146)

Amid the action and reaction of so dense a swarm of humanity, every possible combination of events may be expected to take place, and many a little problem will be presented which may be striking and bizarre without being criminal.

The Greek Interpreter (page 147)

1. D; 2. B; 3. A; 4. C

Motel Hideout (page 148)

The thief is in room 45.

Coded Note (page 149)

Abbey Grange, Marsham, Kent

My dear Mr. Holmes:

I should be very glad of your immediate assistance in what promises to be a most remarkable case. It is something quite in your line. Except for releasing the lady I will see that everything is kept exactly as I have found it, but I beg you not to lose an instant, as it is difficult to leave Sir Eustace there.

Yours faithfully,

Stanley Hopkins.

Story: The Adventure of the Abbey Grange

Irene Adler (page 150)

1. B; 2. D; 3. C; 4. A

Overheard Information (Part II) (page 152)

1. Zero $5 bills, 100 $10 bills, 35 $20 bills, zero $50 bills, 60 $100 bills

2. 03-21-17

3. Thursday at 6 PM

Answer Key

The Adventure of the Speckled Band
(Part II) (page 154)

1. c; 2. b; 3. d; 4. b

Bank Mayhem (page 155)

The answer is 99.

Watson's Schooldays (page 156)

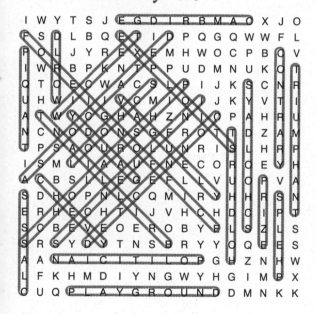

Fingerprint Match (page 158)

The matching pairs are: A and M; B and G; C and P; D and K; E and J; F and O; H and I; L and N

In the End (page 159)

"If my record were closed tonight I could still SURVEY it with EQUANIMITY. The air of London is the SWEETER for my PRESENCE. In over a thousand cases I am not aware that I have ever used my powers upon the wrong side. Of late I have been TEMPTED to look into the problems FURNISHED by nature rather than those more SUPERFICIAL ones for which our ARTIFICIAL state of SOCIETY is responsible. Your MEMOIRS will draw to an end, Watson, upon the day that I crown my career by the CAPTURE or EXTINCTION of the most dangerous and capable criminal in Europe."

Story: The Final Problem

In the Country (page 160)

"Do you know, Watson," said he, "that it is one of the curses of a mind with a turn like mine that I must look at everything with reference to my own special subject. You look at these scattered houses, and you are impressed by their beauty. I look at them, and the only thought which comes to me is a feeling of their isolation and of the impunity with which crime may be committed there.. . . . They always fill me with a certain horror. It is my belief, Watson, founded upon my experience, that the lowest and vilest alleys in London do not present a more dreadful record of sin than does the smiling and beautiful countryside."

Story: The Adventure of the Copper Beeches

What Changed? (Part II) (page 162)

The meat fork disappeared.

Answer Key

Motel Hideout (page 163)

The thief is in room 54.

A Range of Cases (page 164)

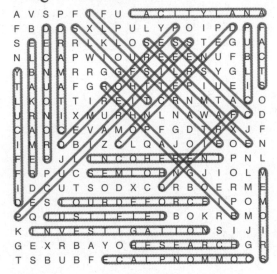

Sherlock (page 166)

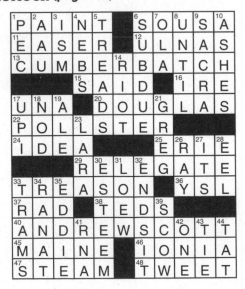

Police Station Shenanigans (page 168)

The answer is 42.

A Scandal in Bohemia (page 169)

1. B; 2. D; 3. A; 4. C

The Showdown (page 170)

Now, if I could have done this without the knowledge of Professor Moriarty, all would have been well. But he was too wily for that. He saw every step which I took to draw my toils round him. Again and again he strove to break away, but I as often headed him off. I tell you, my friend, that if a detailed account of that silent contest could be written, it would take its place as the most brilliant bit of thrust-and-parry work in the history of detection. Never have I risen to such a height, and never have I been so hard pressed by an opponent. He cut deep, and yet I just undercut him. This morning the last steps were taken, and three days only were wanted to complete the business. I was sitting in my room thinking the matter over, when the door opened and Professor Moriarty stood before me.

Story: The Final Problem